MEMORIES O1

AND BEYOND

By

MARJORY G. HARRIS

ISBN: 1-55212-419-3
First published: September 2000

All photos were taken by M.G. Harris with her own camera.

Printed in Canada

Canadian Cataloguing in Publication Data

Harris, Marjory G., 1908-
    Memories of the Moorish world, and beyond

    ISBN 1-55212-419-3

    1. Harris, Marjory G., 1908- --Journeys. 2. Voyages around the world.
I. Title.
G440.H37 2000   910.4'1   C00-910761-4

TRAFFORD

This book was published *on-demand* in cooperation with Trafford Publishing.
On-demand publishing is a unique process and service of making a book available for retail sale to the public taking advantage of on-demand manufacturing and Internet marketing.
On-demand publishing includes promotions, retail sales, manufacturing, order fulfilment, accounting and collecting royalties on behalf of the author.

Suite 6E, 2333 Government St., Victoria, B.C. V8T 4P4, CANADA
Phone   250-383-6864   Toll-free   1-888-232-4444 (Canada & US)
Fax   250-383-6804   E-mail   sales@trafford.com
Web site   www.trafford.com   TRAFFORD PUBLISHING IS A DIVISION OF TRAFFORD HOLDINGS LTD.
Trafford Catalogue #00-0084   www.trafford.com/robots/00-0084.html

10   9   8   7   6   5   4   3

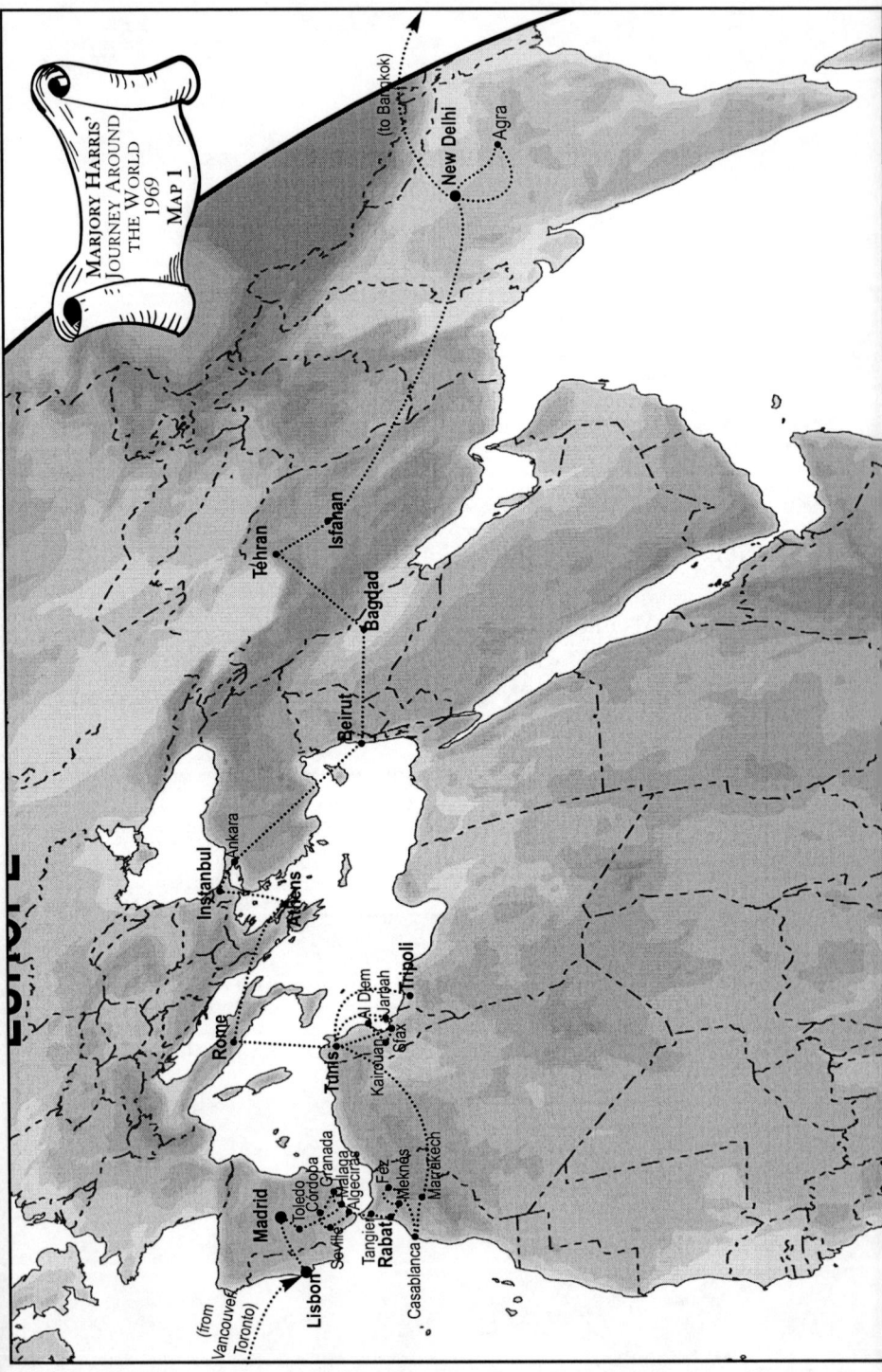

MARJORY HARRIS'
JOURNEY AROUND
THE WORLD
1969
MAP 1

MARJORY HARRIS'
JOURNEY AROUND
THE WORLD
1969
MAP 2

Vancouver

San Francisco

PACIFIC
OCEAN

Hawaii

Tokyo

Hong Kong

Bangkok

(from Isfahan)

*To all of my grandchildren
and great grandchildren*

Oceans of love

Granny Marjory

Many people helped bring this book together:
my editor, Sheilagh Simpson,
my designer, Filipe Figueira,
my secretary, Maureen Salmon,
my assistant, Jenny Liu,
and Katherine Davison, who encouraged me to
buy my computer and start writing.

MEMORIES OF THE MOORISH WORLD

MAy 5th, 1969

I was in the Vancouver Airport saying goodbye to my family and friends and showing them my chain of air tickets. A sixty-one year old grandmother, I was joining a group going off to visit the Moorish World: an overnight in Lisbon, Portugal, then Spain, Morocco, Tunisia, and Libya. Then I was going, alone, beyond the Moorish World: to Italy, Greece, Turkey, Lebanon, and Iran. Iran is almost half way around the world and I could return to Vancouver via India, Thailand, Hong Kong, Japan, and Honolulu for only an additional seventy-five dollars, I was, of course, doing that!

The trip promised to be interesting, relaxing, and fun. I had met most of the tour group at lectures held at the University of British Columbia (UBC) during the previous winter. Different professors explained about the Moorish World: the geography, the history, religions, and the Roman ruins in that area. Our group consisted of two professors, one tour leader, and the twenty-five people who had taken the course at UBC.

1

Travelling as a group meant that all meals, hotel reservations, and transportation arrangements would be looked after. None of us would have to carry vouchers, plane tickets, or money for meals. This put great pressure on the tour director, but she was a capable and experienced young woman, so the rest of us could relax and have fun. It was one long party.

Lisbon, PORTUGAL, and SPAIN

We landed in Lisbon, Portugal, and spent the night in a pleasant hotel on the main street in the centre of town. There was a tour to a Moorish castle, but I declined to go as I had seen it with the family about ten years before. It was very interesting to hear that they still had a white peacock in the roof garden.

The next morning we had a short flight to Madrid, Spain. The hotel was conveniently near the centre of tourist sights and several of us walked around looking at shops, parks, office buildings, statues, and hotels. We stopped at a sidewalk cafe for a cool drink. That evening we were gathering for dinner when we found that the dining room did not open until nine o'clock! Some went to the bar. But some of us were hungry, and we went out looking for a restaurant. They all seemed to be closed. We finally found one with a light on, so we tried the door. The tables were set, so we rattled the door and knocked. There was no sign of life. We rattled the handle again. At that moment, a window above us banged open and an angry woman shook her fist at us yelling something in Spanish, which sounded like "Police". As she kept on shouting, we decided that we were not so hungry after all. A crowd was gathering, so we slipped away, and were glad to get back to the hotel and have a long cool drink. The dinner had been ordered, so we were served promptly at nine p.m.

At nine the next morning, the tour bus arrived to take us to the King Charles III's palace for the morning and, after lunch, the Prado. The palace was full of beautiful furniture and pictures, but to some of us the most interesting parts were the clock collection and the heating system. The clocks were presented to the various kings on different occasions, and dated back for centuries. There were grandfather clocks, tiny bedroom ones, some in carvings of animals, and many others. They came from England, France, Italy, Japan, China, and other countries.

My friend from home, Anne, and I had gone with the guide to see the back halls—another marvel of the palace—and the 'jars'. I had often wondered what the many six to ten foot decorated jars were in the corners of so many rooms. In the back, however, they were just like old-fashioned black metal furnaces with false fronts. The servants must have been constantly going into the back halls to feed wood and coal to these furnaces. But once we touched them, we knew that were real! And When Anne and I came out to join the group, we looked at each other, and were surprised to find black smudges on our hands and faces.

The visit to the Prado, an enormous art gallery, was educational, beautiful, and exhausting. It is one of the largest galleries in the world. Some paintings were by world famous artists, others were by unfamiliar painters. My favourite ones were by an artist named Velazquez. The most prolific painter was El Greco, a Cretan-born, Spanish artist who had lived in Toledo. We were to visit Toledo the next day and learn more about him. There was also a museum in the Prado that displayed antique furniture, vases, and other historic items.

Our next bus trip, south to Toledo, started at eight the next morning. The ancient city was on a triangular shaped promontory. It was a fabulous fortress with two vertical cliffs jutting up from the Tagus River, and a steep slope on the third side. The streets in the old town at the top were too narrow for our bus, so we had to walk to the first point of interest, a steel factory. It specialized in producing 'the best knives in the world'. The process of producing sharp knives, scissors, and in the old days, swords, was so intriguing that we found it hard to leave. Some of us bought souvenir letter openers or tiny nail scissors.

The walk up to the main cathedral through the winding narrow streets was rough. The cathedral specialized in El Greco paintings. The annex next door was spectacular, with many more of his artistic achievements. The most spectacular was a huge mural depicting the end of the life of Christ, the Garden of Gethsemane, the Last Supper, and the crucifixion. It was an overwhelming piece of art. We spent a long time gazing from one end to the other. I was deeply impressed by this painting, but made uncomfortable, not only by the tragic sadness, but also because I felt the figures were almost unreal. The figures seemed elongated, as if distorted by a mirror. We finally tore ourselves away to see the house where El Greco had lived. When we reached the door, a sign read 'closed'! We wanted to walk back to the Parador where we had been for lunch, but there was no time. The Parador was one of the many old historic buildings that the government had rebuilt into attractive inns. There were many around Spain. The walk back to the bus was tiring. We were all happy to sit back and enjoy the pretty country as we drove back to Madrid.

We flew south the following day to Malaga, a charming city on the Mediterranean not far east of Gibraltar. There we had a local guide. After a brief tour of the city, we drove up into the mountains toward Granada. I never thought of southern Spain as being mountainous, but it is. It took our old bus a long time going up one switchback after another. Suddenly we were there!

From our hotel we had a good view of the Alhambra, the famous Moorish palace in Granada—an elaborate, ornate complex of living quarters, courtyards, gardens, fountains, reception rooms, and mosques with minarets. We spent most of the day in the Alhambra with local guides, wandering in and out of the labyrinth of rooms, courtyards, and mosques. The flat roofs, the elaborate carvings, and ornate decorations were surprising, and awe inspiring! The building decorations were interesting because there were no human figures, no animal replicas, and no flower decorations. All decorations or carvings were geometric. The only curves were to be found in the Arabic writing, usually a quotation from the Koran, the holy book of the Moslems. The Alhambra gardens were colourful with a profusion of flowers of every variety: carnations, impatiens, snapdragons, and bougainvilleas growing everywhere. There were many blossoming trees and shrubs. The fountains, pools, and connecting canals flowed from one courtyard to another. The builders used a great many coloured tiles, particularly in the mosques and minarets.

Our guide arranged for us to see flamenco dancing at the outdoor theatre in the Gypsy village down in the valley below our hotel. About half of us decided to go. The Gypsy dancers were beautiful with dark flashing eyes. The clicking of their castanets and the tapping of their heels added extra zest to the peppy music. The women's long colourful dresses with the swirling skirts added a colourful contrast to the more sombre costumes of the male dancers. It was a lovely evening. We all went back to our hotel swirling our skirts and clicking our heels to the rhythm of the lively tunes, which we were still humming. In the morning, with one last look at the marvelous Alhambra, we set off for Cordoba—our next rendezvous with Moorish architecture.

After a short trip over more mountains we were in a wide fertile river valley, and in Cordoba. The main mosque was huge, covering about the area of a city block. As we went through the gate into the compound, the blossoming trees softened the straight lines of the pillars, which were geometrically spaced in all directions. When the Moors were eventually defeated and returned to Africa, the Spaniards built a Roman Catholic cathedral in the centre of the mosque!

After we had toured the elaborately decorated cathedral, we boarded our bus and drove down the valley to the lovely city of Seville. It was a profusion of brilliant colours, with trees blossoming and window boxes overflowing with flowers of all kinds on every balcony and every porch. Looking down the main street past the lovely houses, we could see the Guadalquivir River, which is navigable up to the harbour. When we climbed the Giralda Tower, we could see the river winding across the enormous lowland swamp and farmland to the north, and to the south, towards Cadiz on the Mediterranean. On these lowlands people had filled in marshes and dredged out rivers to make room for the magnificent World's Fair, which would be held the following year. We stayed that night in an old but cozy little inn, falling asleep to the sounds of flamenco dancing heard in the distance.

The mist over the lowlands in the morning heat gave a refreshing look to the harsh landscape as we set off on our day's adventure. We followed the river south, towards Cadiz. Then we turned east, to Algeciras, where we'd catch the ferry to Tangier. The ferry was waiting for us at the dock. Our bus was going with us, but we could not stay in it, as we had to go through customs and immigration. The ferry was large, almost as big as an ocean liner.

Leaving Spain behind, many of us felt regrets because we had not seen more and learned more of that lovely country. As the ferry left the dock, turning into the Mediterranean, we looked forward to seeing Gibraltar. As the big ship rounded the Cape of Gibraltar, we were impressed by the magnitude of the rock, and by its fortifications. We headed west, toward the Atlantic and our next port, Tangier, Morocco, on the north coast of Africa.

Saying "goodbye" to my grandchildren, showing them the chain of around the world tickets.

Gate to Alhambra in Granada, Spain.

Typical architecture in Seville.

MOROCCO

Tangier has a very international history. It was first conquered by the Moors who swept across north Africa, crossed into Spain as far north as Valladolid, then retreated to Cordoba and Grenada, where they ruled for four hundred years. Tangier was also conquered and ruled over by the Spanish, French, and British. For a few years Tangier was an independent country, but it is now a province of Morocco. Rabat is the capital city of Morocco, and Casablanca a major Atlantic seaport.

Tangier was a surprising city. The first shock was how foreign, to me, the people looked and dressed. Most of the men wore long flowing robes, and some had long white costumes fitted like a ladies dress, with white pillbox-type hats. Mixed in with this conglomeration were the desert tribal Berbers with their brilliant striped robes and flowing head and neck coverings, called *jilbab*, held on with bright corded bands, like a crown around the head. There were enough people in western clothes to make us feel welcome.

When we landed on the wharf, we were gathered together to hear that there had been a change in our plans. One of our travel companions, Mrs. Parker, had an infected leg and required medical care in a hospital. The Parkers would have to stay in Tangier for about a week. This meant a complicated re-arrangement of their tickets and hotel reservations. Our tour guide would make all of the arrangements. So we were to be on our own for two hours, and then report back to the bus for further instructions. Anne and I decided to see some of the city.

Tangier had grown up around the harbour, spreading out over the hills giving the harbour and city a unique and cozy appearance. The variety of architecture reflected the cultures of the different countries that had ruled the area for so many years. As we walked along a street, we would come to a typical English manor house, then a Spanish mansion, or a French villa. The Spanish, French, and English influence was everywhere. You could hear it and see it on the billboard and street signs, and on the names of the stores, the streets, and in the newspapers.

The water supply did not seem to be a problem here as the numerous Moorish houses with their flat roofs and courtyards had extensive pools and fountains.

We were tired and thirsty, so we decided to find out what the Café Lafayette could offer us. Inside, we realized that there were only men there drinking. We did not find out until later that it was a bar, not a cafe, and for men only! We had seated ourselves at a table for two, and did not understand why all eyes were looking at us. The barman was a true international, and in excellent English, with a decidedly French accent, asked, "You are a visitor? May I offer you a leetle refreshment? A glass of wine or an aperitif?" We asked for a gin and tonic. "But of course, a long cool drink for the Mesdames." We did not linger over our drink, but walked out as gracefully as possible. Deciding that we had had enough experiences for the day, we found our way back to the bus.

The news was good. The Parkers were settled into their comfortable hotel and arrangements for medical care were finalized. We were to start for Rabat in twenty minutes. It was getting dark as we left Tangier, so we did not see much of the country, and were happy to arrive at our pleasant hotel.

At eleven the next morning, we set off to have a guided tour of the Imperial Palace of His Majesty, the King of Morocco. The guard at the high gate, which opened between high walls into the palace grounds, had never heard of Canada, and he refused to let us in. After much telephoning we were allowed to enter the outer courtyard. We waited there for a long time, milling around like a flock of lost sheep, while the local guide disappeared in search of permission to enter the palace. We wandered around the courtyard admiring the fascinating array of unusual buildings spreading out in all directions. The elaborate designs of the fretwork that filled in the openings instead of glass were intricate and geometric, yet useful, as they allowed light and air in, but gave privacy. No dice. The local guide apologized, murmuring about misunderstandings, etc., and led us out the outer gate, and back onto the bus. It was very disappointing. It would have been nice to see what the inside was like with people living in those lovely buildings. Although we did not see the Rabat port, we were told it was a busy one.

On our way to Meknes the next day, we stopped to see the Roman ruins of Velubolis, which date back to the first century. We wondered why such a big city should have been built on this large flat plain—one of many questions to which we did not find answers. Many large pillars were still standing, but it was hard to visualize people living there. We got back in the bus and continued east across the plain to Meknes.

Meknes is both an old city and a modern one, both inside a high wall. Entering through the gate was a nerve-wracking experience! There were no traffic signals. Old cars, new cars, trucks, camels, goats, men on horseback, and our bus all seemed to be going in different directions. When I had travelled in southern Africa, I had seen a sign saying that the elephant had the right of way. I did not see any signs saying that camels had the right of way here, but they certainly acted as if they did. They sauntered across in front of us, with their heads held high, ignoring everyone and everything. We finally inched our way through the old city and into the 'new' city, where we were to spend the night. At the hotel they explained why there was such a traffic jam at the gate: there was to be a fair and horse show the following day, and we were attending.

The next day, after entering the fair grounds, Anne and I became separated from the group and found ourselves surrounded by big fierce looking men and restless stomping horses. As we looked around for some way to escape, we saw a fair haired man easing his way through the crowd toward us asking in English, "Can I help you?" We explained that Anne had been admiring the bay mare, and the men had surrounded us. "But," he said, "they think that you want to buy it. Just tell them that it is too big, and I will explain this to them." We energetically waved our arms around saying, "TOO BIG". The Englishman patted the horse saying nice words about the beauty of this horse, and suggested that he might be interested in buying it, and that he had a pony that he thought we might like. We shook hands with the owner, and followed our new friend out of the circle of horsetraders.

As he escorted us to a quieter area, he asked, "What are you young ladies doing wandering around dressed like this, unescorted?" We explained that we were with a group touring the Moorish world. After we had walked in silence for some time, we came to a gate. He pointed to a viewing stand saying, "I think your group is up there watching the Berber shooting contest. I hope you enjoy the rest of your journey." We shook hands with him, and thanked him for his kindness in rescuing us. We went up to the viewing stand to join the group. The contest had already started, and riders on galloping horses raced by, one by one, with rifles ready to shoot at floating targets. Number three shot down two targets, number five only one. And so it went, until they had all gone around the track three times, and a winner proclaimed. The winner paraded around, then a flower wreath was placed around the horse's neck, and a medal and a cash prize given to the marksman. It had been an exciting contest, and we all cheered for the winner.

When we arrived back at our hotel some of our group decided to walk over to the railway station to see the trains. Meknes was an important junction with trains connecting Tangier, Rabat, and Fez with Casablanca and Marrakech. Some of us thought that it would be pleasant to go to Casablanca and Marrakech by train rather than by our old bus. However, we were due to go north to Fez the next morning, in our old bus.

That night, I wished that I was anywhere but in this old hotel. I had to share a very small room with Gerda, who grumbled constantly about the inadequate bathroom facilities and about the lack of air-conditioning. The beds were so close together that we had to take turns getting out of bed. It was very hot and very stuffy. (The window opened onto a small light well, which let in the unpleasant noise and smell from the kitchen). Neither of us slept much that night, and we were not on very friendly terms in the morning.

On our way to Fez, we were stopped at a crossroad and had to wait in line. When we got out to see what was causing the delay, we were thrilled to see the boat Ra being taken on a truck to the sea. The Norwegian seafarer Thor, Heyerdahl, had built it. He also built, and sailed a reed boat, the Kon Tiki, across the Pacific to Easter Island to prove that the natives of South America could have reached the South Pacific islands. Some people have more courage than others. He did prove that the people in prehistoric times could have populated the Americas. It was very strange to see a boat made of reeds going down a highway in semi-desert country.

When we arrived at our hotel in Fez, we were pleasantly surprised to find that it was a charming little inn on the top of a hill overlooking this ancient town. After lunch we set out to explore the souk, a Moslem market place. The streets were too narrow for any vehicle to drive through, so we left our bus at the gate. The town was built in a hollow surrounded by an ancient wall. The streets were steep and narrow, and the cobblestones were worn and uneven. It was hot and very smelly. If a donkey came along with his bulging load on each side, a person had to back up into a shop to let him pass.

In spite of the heat, the rough walking, and the smell, we had a wonderful time shopping. The shops were full of fascinating things. There was a glass blower making beautiful glass ornaments, and practical and pretty cups and bowls of all shapes and sizes. The jewelry artisan was setting jewels in bracelets, necklaces, earrings, and rare ornaments. Leather was the specialty of Morocco, and Fez was the tanning centre. Every imaginable thing that could be made out of leather was there in the leather shops, from hand tooled desk sets to shoes and jackets. We all watched them tanning the hides and marveled at the soft pliable leather.

Handicrafts of all kinds were tempting us, including kitchen-wares and bedroom lamps. Wrecked car bodies were being beaten into pails. We all seemed to be in a buying mood. One person would go back to buy a sweater, and another bought leather sandals. Some found the jewelery irresistible. We had examined every shop down one 'street', up the other, and in hidden alleys, disliking the smelly, bumpy crowded streets, but loving the beauty of the things in the shops.

We gathered at the bus, and proudly displayed our purchases. It had been a happy adventure.

In the morning we set off for a one-night stopover in Casablanca, a very cosmopolitan city. While exploring Casablanca, we found a very fashionable restaurant, and some of us decided to treat our-selves to a special dinner that evening. Seven of us met in the lobby and decided to skip the cocktail hour and try Moroccan wine with our dinner. The menu was international, the food was delicious, and the waiters were experts. Some liked the wine, others did not. It was a gala evening. We felt as if we had dined at a posh New York night club. We had taken a taxi to the restaurant, but we walked the long way back to the hotel. I enjoyed the fun of having a room to myself, which was relatively quiet, in spite of the trains and the ships' whistles.

The following morning, we were all up early and looking forward to our trip through the Atlas Mountains to Marrakech. Marrakech was on the edge of the Sahara, and it was exciting to be approaching that great desert! As we travelled, the vegetation became sparser, with brown grass meadows and fewer trees. Off in the distance, at the top of a grassy hill, we saw three camels silhouetted against the blue sky. It was a dramatic sight. At that time, I was just beginning to know a little about camels: they can go for long periods of time without replenishing their water supply, and they are invaluable for transporting people and freight across the vast desert.

The Atlas Mountains were not very high or steep, and soon the land became more like a desert. In the distance we could see Marrakech! This was where civilization ended. Here was the end of our highway, the railway, or any other means of transportation. Airlines transferred cargo and passengers. You could sense the excitement of people planning to go out into the vast, mostly uncharted desert, usually in convoys. The smaller planes did noble jobs transferring goods and people to distant oases.

Before we settled into our hotel, our driver took us into the desert for about twenty miles over a couple of hills, and then stopped on the crest of a sand dune. When we got out of the bus, we wandered around and up the road. We could see nothing but sand. The area was not flat, like the prairies. There were only sand dunes, then more sand dunes as far as the eye could see in all directions! There was only sky, sun, and sand! Our little road lost itself beyond the second sand dune! We had to drive on for about a mile where a track turned west in order to turn around and return to Marrakech. We were overwhelmed with the vastness of the Sahara.

The next morning, we were eager to explore the fabulous city of Marrakech. The Sultan's palace was enormous, covering about four city blocks. The walls that surrounded the palace were eight or ten feet high, and once you were through the gate you knew that you were in a different world. There were big courtyards and little courtyards. A labyrinth of fountains and waterways flowed from one courtyard through the rooms and into another. Every 'window' had a different fancy design—dainty filigree plaster work, all geometric. There was pretty tile work with generous amounts of gold and silver decorations. We visited other palaces that were not only older, but obviously not lived in or cared for. And we visited museums. I have a distaste for 'doing' museums. I think it is almost useless to go 'through' a museum, unless you have time to read and study what an item is, where it came from, and why it is a museum artifact. However, I do go through museums, figuring that perhaps a little of this exhibit and a little of that exhibit is better than hours spent on one thing.

Arrangements had been made for our group to have cocktails before dinner at a little cafe on the city square, and to go to a roof garden to view a daily custom that was also the event of the day. It was the custom in Marrakech for everyone to meet in the city square at five or six o'clock. It was like a fair: everyone was in a festive mood. There were booths with snake charmers, magicians, musicians, and hawkers everywhere. There were groups of men who seemed to be discussing serious business, telling jokes, or just greeting friends. We watched the crowds until it was getting dark, and the people were bidding each other farewell. It was cooling off on our lovely roof garden, and we were reluctant to leave. Back at the hotel, some of us took a last stroll through the beautiful garden with flowers and palm trees glowing in the night lights.

We left Marrakech the next morning with many regrets. I would like to have seen the small caravans starting off across the desert. I would like to have asked someone how they kept the roads clear after a sand storm. And I wondered how they got water, and how they produced electricity.

The drive back to Casablanca seemed endless. We had a late lunch there, and then caught the plane for Tunisia, with a brief stop in Algeria. We could not get off the plane there because of fighting, and flew on to Tunisia.

Roman ruins at Velubolis.

Thor Heyerdhal's Ra on its way to the sea. He had taken the Kon Tiki across the Pacific.

I kept my distance from the snake charmer in Marrakech.

The lively street dancers in the streets of Tunis.

Marjory enjoying the colourful flowers in a garden in Tunis.

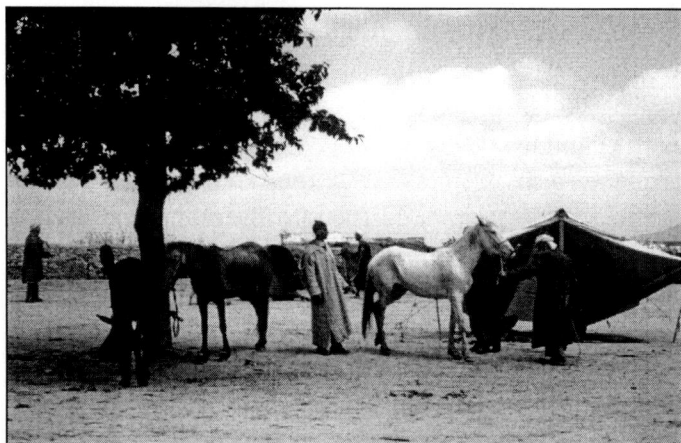

Horses relaxing after the show in the countryside near Kairouan.

TUNISIA, and Tripoli, LIBYA

We arrived at our hotel after dark. I always think it is a shame to drive through a new city after dark, because it is difficult to get much of an impression through a bus window at high speed. Our hotel was small, white, and clean, on a pretty tree-lined boulevard conveniently near the centre of Tunis, the capital of Tunisia.

When we ventured out in the brilliant morning sunshine to explore the city, we were pleasantly surprised. Everything seemed to be white. The buildings were painted white, and by law, they must renew the paint every few years. The men wore white, either Arab robes or western 'tropics'. Even the women wore white. Everyone seemed to be happy and friendly. Everyone and everything was dressed up to enjoy the lovely summer sunshine. It was such a pleasure to walk along the shady tree-lined streets.

Tunis had been badly damaged during the Second World War. The Germans had occupied Tunisia, so when the Allied troops closed in, there was fierce fighting and terrible destruction. It was here that the Germans were forced into the Cape. They had no way to retreat, no way to get supplies, and were forced to surrender. After the war Tunis had to be rebuilt—thus the wider streets and boulevards. The wide streets and modern buildings made us feel more cheerful. There was much laughter, telling of jokes, and clowning. We all seemed to be in a party mood!

We visited the Roman ruins in Carthage, which seemed to be part of the city. We had one serious lecture about Carthage, the Roman Empire, and the conquering Moors. Then a tour with a local guide who made it very real, and gave us a picture of life as it was then.

One day Anne and I were walking along a side street, and were interested to see an elderly gentleman sitting at a table in front of his store writing with an old fashioned pen and a bottle of ink. He seemed to be writing backwards. He looked up at us, and smiled. He stood up, bowed, and asked if he could help us. We were embarrassed and surprised that he spoke such perfect English. "I am sorry to interrupt you, but you seemed to be writing backwards," I said. "Yes, it is the Arabic way." He explained that he was a scribe, and that letter writing was his profession. "There are many illiterate people in this country, so I write letters, personal or business." He bowed again, and invited us in to see his little shop.

It was like a small stationery store. There were samples of letters, business forms and documents, official seals, pens, pencils, and other items. He continued, "You are surprised at my English, my blue eyes, and my shop? Yes? Well, I was born in Sfax, a city south of here. My mother was English and my father Tunisian, Moslem. They were both educated people, so they insisted that I should go to university. I taught school for a while, then decided that there was a great need for a scribe. So here I am."

He asked us where we came from and why we were in Tunis. He was very interested in our plans to travel south, and gave us suggestions about what to see and do in his home town, Sfax. As we thanked him and were leaving, he called after us, "Do not forget to visit the university; it is one of the oldest in the world."

We thanked him again, and asked if he would allow us to take his picture. He bowed and said, "But, yes, of course. But do not go around taking pictures of people or animals, because many of our people believe that the eye of the camera is evil and will take away their soul. Be very careful. Mobs have seized cameras and trampled on them, very angrily. Please be very careful." We thanked him again, took his picture and left. He was such a good-looking man, so kind and serene. I will always remember him.

After we left him, we met some of the group, and went to a roof garden where they served mint tea, and where there was a good view of the city. That night we went to a night club. Refreshments were served. Then with clanging cymbals, the floor show came on. Wow! Belly dancers with jewels sparkling in their navels glided on to the stage! I had seen floor shows in Paris, New York, and Los Angeles, but seldom one as shocking—in a country where most of the women had to cover themselves from head to toe, somehow I had not expected to see so much bare flesh! Their sheer silk pantaloons were tied around their ankles with flashing bracelets. A semi see-through blouse covered the top half of their wiggling bodies. Bracelets glittered at their wrists, and jewels flashed in their black hair, dazzling the eye. They were good dancers, and the audience loved the show! Need I add that most of the audience were men. In my travels I saw many other belly dancers, but never again felt so shocked. When the floor show was over we walked back to the hotel.

We left Tunis in the morning in a comfortable new bus. Our local guide was very friendly, helpful, and full of interesting facts and legends about his country. He would point out a farm, telling us that one raised cows for the production of milk, but another raised them only for beef. Over there the government was drilling, not for oil, but for water. We arrived in Sfax early in the afternoon, and had a tour of the city before dinner and a quick tour of the harbour before checking into our hotel.

The large harbour was a surprise, not only because of the size, but the numbers of big ships loading and unloading cargo of all kinds. Here were big freighters that probably came to Vancouver, yet I had never heard of this city. Perhaps during the war battles were lost and won here. However, this would not have given the city of Sfax a reputation of being an international commercial shipping centre!

The city itself was an interesting mixture of the old and the new. There were tall air-conditioned office buildings, apartments, and streets of open stores with shutters that were pulled down at closing time. The parks were full of shade trees, palm trees, fountains, and tiled resting areas.

We left Sfax in the morning, and, because the scribe had suggested that we see his university, Kairouan University, we detoured inland to see it. The university did not impress us; some of the buildings were obviously very old, but most of them were contemporary.

Within a few miles of the university, we saw the Egbert rug warehouse which impressed us very much. The rugs were so beautiful that many of our group bought them! Evidently Kairouan was a centre of rug weaving and manufacturing; they made rugs of all kinds. Those who bought large ones had to arrange for the rugs to be shipped to Vancouver. The salesman knew his business, and papers were quickly signed. Then we were off to a different kind of horse show than the one we had seen in Meknes. This was more of a family affair.

Shelters had been arranged around a large oval racetrack. The audience consisted of men, women, and children crowding under the shelters in the shade, if they could find a space. I would call this display acrobatic horse riding. Riders would do all kinds of tricks. Men would ride backwards, then flip over the horse and touch the ground on one side, then flip over to touch the ground on the other side while the horse was galloping. One man stood on his head and did not fall as he flipped back onto the saddle!

Between shows, there were clowns, children riding ponies, ice-cream vendors, Coca-Cola in the bottle, and strange things looking like hot dogs. The horses were big handsome brutes, rather frightening from our low-level vantage spot. It was an impressive example of superb horsemanship. We all enjoyed the afternoon, although some of us got severely sunburned.

I was happy to have a single room, although small, with the window looking out on a wee courtyard with a fountain, pretty tiled walks and lots of shade trees, palms and shrubs.

We continued travelling south, on the main highway to Jarbah Island. This day's trip was very different. One reason was that we took another detour — because the Roman ruins expert on our tour insisted we see this jewel in the desert, a small replica of the Rome Colosseum! Djem was built hundreds of years ago. The story told to us was that the rocks were brought from Rome by ship, and because of hostile tribes, were hauled twenty miles inland through a tunnel. To us that seemed to be a futile arrangement. But perhaps they were not so stupid, because the Romans were expert at building rock works, and this was preferable to shifting sands and hostile tribes. They had built aqueducts all over the known world to carry water for domestic purposes and for irrigating the land. The sandstorms had done plenty of damage, but had failed to obliterate this colossal example of Roman engineering skill and superb workmanship. We were very impressed but puzzled: why here? With this thought uppermost in our minds, we climbed into the bus, returned to the highway, and headed south. We never did find out why.

Another reason the day was very different was because we visited a camel farm, south of Sfax. But it took us a long time to get there, and the country became more and more desert-like. Although I could never love camels, I have always been fascinated by these curious animals. They had camel races at the farm, but not that day. Instead, they were offering to take any of us for a ride around the oval. My friend, Anne, and I were the only daring ones to accept the offer.

I had bought a Berber costume—just the head dress and the top shirt—so I put that on for the ride. The camel knelt down on all four legs and I had to climb onto an unfamiliar saddle. The camel startled me by getting up jerkily on front legs first, then hind legs. I felt sky-high looking down on all those people. I do not know how camel riders can endure long days in such discomfort. When we were back at the starting point, the nasty animal suddenly dropped down on his front legs. I jerked forward, almost over his head, but managed to grab around his neck, and as he lowered his hind legs, I slid ungracefully to solid ground! The guide rescued me, but my pride was bruised. I took off my Berber outfit and sat down in a spectator's seat just in time to see Anne arrive back and slide gracefully to the ground! There were gales of laughter and plenty of joking about the blonde camel riders.

"Perhaps you would like to join a caravan and ride our camels across the Sahara to Timbuktu?" said the tour guide. We thanked him, but "no," we said, and said goodbye to our friendly camel farmer, instructing the guide to thank him for us, as he could not speak English.

Further south, on the main coastal highway, we turned inland again into a deep valley. On one side there was a high cliff, and paths led up to holes in the rock-like side. The guide told us that people, even now, lived in the caves! Perhaps with little or no rain and continual heat—up to 120 degrees fahrenheit in the day—the caves would be cool. Was this how the original cavemen lived? We were all silent for a long time.

We had almost reached the end of our southern tour, and, as we turned east around the bay, we could see the Island of Jarbah, with the long, low bridge leading to it. The first part of the bridge was over mudflats, probably covered with water at high tide. The whole bridge stretched for about half a mile before rising up over the deep channel, then on to the island. The island was not very large, about five miles wide and ten miles long. There was a modern motel on the eastern beach. As we were all anxious to have a swim in the Mediterranean, the tour of the island was brief.

The most interesting sight on the Island of Jarbah was the method they used to get water out of a well. The well was about three feet in diameter, and had some sort of a pulley arrangement that pulled the pail of water up out of the well and dumped it into a trough. The power to do this was provided by a combination of ropes and pulleys attached to a camel! The camel would stride down the hill, pulling the bucket of water up out of the well. As he turned at the bottom of the hill, the bucket would dump the water over the edge into the cement culvert. When he started up the hill, the bucket would drop down to the bottom and fill with water. As the camel went around the top of the well and started down the hill, he would be pulling the bucket up out of the well again. We watched this unusual generation of power for some time.

As we checked into the charming motel on the eastern shore of the island, we looked with excitement at the beautiful sandy Mediterranean beach. The last few days had been very hot, and we looked forward to a refreshing swim. It did not take very long to change into our bathing suits and race to test the water. One by one we all tested the water, and found it fine. But a strong, very cold north wind chilled us, and made the sea rough. We ran back to the wind breaks, and had second thoughts about going for a swim. Some hardy souls did swim, but most of us just plunged in, ran out, and huddled behind the wind breaks. We were all soon back on the patio, out of the wind, and in the warm sunshine.

As we relaxed on the patio, we looked across the sea toward Libya, and speculated about the reasons for closing the border between Tunisia and Libya, about thirty miles away. Tripoli, the capital of Libya — and our last 'Moorish' destination — was about one hundred miles east of the border. But we had to fly back to Tunis, before flying on to Tripoli the next day. We were urged to pack only enough for a one-night stay in Tripoli; when we returned to Tunis, we'd be flying to Rome, and then home to Vancouver.

The others would be flying home to Vancouver. I was staying in Rome, and completing my around the world trip.

The flight to Tripoli seemed very short. We settled into our rooms in a very pleasant hotel, and had an hour to spare before the trip to Leptis Magna, the Roman ruins. I decided to go for a walk. The hotel was facing the Mediterranean on a wide boulevard, which swept around the bay to the city harbour. It was too far for me to walk the entire distance, so I rested on a bench admiring the lovely view.

Not far from me was a fruit stand with bananas. I did not have any Libyan money but, as usual, the sight of an American dollar bill worked magic. (I have found this reaction to American currency all over the world.) The vendor wrapped my four bananas in a sheet of newspaper, and I sat on my bench to eat one. As I opened the paper, I was astonished to find that it was a sheet of the London Times. The next surprise was that the bananas were from Costa Rica, in Central America! All of this, while sitting on a bench in Tripoli, in Libya, in North Africa! After eating one of the bananas, I returned to the hotel to tell my friends about my international exchange, all for one American dollar!

The bus was soon at the door waiting to take us to the centuries old Roman ruins. We left the city suburbs, passed through some farmland and undeveloped desert, and finally arrived at Leptis Magna. There was a guide at the gate to explain how the Romans built the city, why they built on that spot, and how they lived. These ruins were the best preserved and the most realistic example of Roman ways of living that I have seen. I followed the crowd along the avenues, admiring the excellent tile work and the pillars and walls still standing. Then the heat overwhelmed me. I went back to the guide's office looking for a cool spot. I just had to lie down! The tiles outside were blazing hot, but the table inside proved to be a good place to stretch out with my head by the open window where a soft breeze from the sea somewhat revived me. I was not the only one who felt the heat; everyone came back exhausted. The bus was like an oven as we stepped into it for the ride to the airport.

The stewardess could see that some of us were ready to pass out, and brought us ice cold drinks with salt tablets, and bathed our foreheads with cold cloths. She explained that there was a particularly scorching sirocco blowing in off the desert, and that this wind happened only once or twice a year. A short stop in the air-conditioned airport located south of Jarbah helped to revive us. The plane was air-conditioned, too, so we all arrived back in Tunis feeling fine.

That night, we had a special farewell dinner, and went back to our rooms early. We were to catch the six a.m. plane to Rome.

I waved goodbye to the rest of the group at the Rome airport, and watched the plane leave for Vancouver. I sat down on a chair, momentarily bewildered. I'd never felt so alone and so on my own in a foreign city. What was I doing here? Alone in this airport! What was I going to do?

Camel-power well, pulling up the water for irrigation in Jarbah, Tunisia.

The Spanish Steps in Rome, Italy. Where artists displayed the pictures for sale.

Soldiers guarding the King's Palace. The changing of the guards, Athens, Greece.

Rome, ITALY, and Athens, GREECE

I do not know how long it took me to decide what I had to do. I really did not have to worry as I had reservations for hotels and planes to Iran, and beyond.

Suddenly I was hungry. I converted my traveller's cheque into Lira. A one hundred dollar cheque bought thousands of Lira, and I had to sit down to organize this unfamiliar pile of bills. I could smell coffee, so I found the café. Fortunately it was a caféteria, and I was able to order an omelette, toast and coffee. I did feel better.

It is usually easy to find a "taxi" in most airports and in most countries, as the word looks very much the same in most languages. The Hotel Excelsior sounds similar in Italian, so I was soon on my way there. I was delighted with this lovely hotel, and was able to register, presenting my voucher.

"Yes, Madam, we have a reservation for you. A nice room on the fourth floor. A boy will take you up in one minute." It was a relief to be greeted in English.

I was so glad to get to my room that I did not mind that it was an 'old maid special'. This is what I call a room that looks out onto a light well or is tucked in behind an elevator. This one, although small, was comfortable, with an easy chair, desk, writing material, and a luxurious bathroom. I soon settled in and began to organize my money, papers, vouchers, and tickets. After a brief rest and a fresh dress, I found my way to the dining room.

I soon realized that dining rooms were a good place to see people, and I learned to walk in nonchalantly and ask for "a table for one, please"— in the local language, if I could. I spent many happy hours watching people while enjoying a good meal. The menu often had English descriptions for visitors.

After a relaxing nights sleep, I was ready to start out on my own. It was strange to be going on a sightseeing bus with strangers; to be only with people who looked different, and spoke different languages. The guide gave her explanations in French and English. Our first visit was to the Colosseum. I had seen many pictures of it, but none of them had prepared me for the size of the place. It was enormous! I stood in the centre and looked up at the layers of arches with stonework seeming to reach the sky, and I felt very small and unimportant. The guide's voice brought me back to earth. She told us about the heroes who had fought lions or other vicious animals. I walked away from the tragic tales, sat on one of the stone seats, and wondered how they got those huge boulders up over the arches. I had been told that the huge stones were cut to fit on the one below, but how did they get them up? I sat on the cold stone seat wondering why people would build such a colossal structure for such cruel events.

The other passengers from our bus tour were coming up from the dungeons where the Romans had kept the lions and the prisoners. I was glad that I had not gone below. It was nicer to remember the amazing accomplishment of two thousand years ago, instead of the use they made of this Colosseum.

Outside the Colosseum, I asked the guide, "Where is the lady's room?" "Go down the stairs to the right of the entrance, and turn right," she said. I did this, and opened the door on my right. A shiver went through me; I was in a very dark dungeon! I retreated in a hurry, running up the stairs and outside into the bright sunshine. The guide apologized, saying, "The right side of the entrance, going out of the Colosseum."

Our next stop was at the Forum, not far from the Colosseum. It was hard to realize that this was the famous Forum. It looked like a neglected grassy racetrack rather than a place where glittering chariot races were held. But it was thousands of years ago, and neither chariot races nor open markets of olden days were held there any more. The business of buying and selling was conducted in large, impressive commercial buildings. This old market had been used as a place to gather people together for public discussions, political and religious. Now, political debates were held in the city hall or in parliament, and religious matters in the Vatican, and other religious centres.

The bus took us past the United Nations Food and Agricultural Organization (F.A.O.), which was near the Forum. I was glad to see the F.A.O. building because I had been invited to have lunch with Bill Gall, an F.A.O. official, the next day. I'd met him in Vancouver when I was involved with the United Nations International Co-operation Year.

After a brief visit to the Vatican City, the bus took us to a few memorial monuments, fountains, the Villa Borghese Gallery, the museum, and the Spanish Steps.

After lunch, I walked back to the Villa Borghese Gardens, and passed the dozens of sidewalk cafés. They were all very busy. The little bit of sidewalk left for pedestrians was very crowded. Everyone seemed to be in a holiday mood, and did not seem to be in a hurry to find the right café, or they may just have been looking for someone to join them for a drink. This was not the easiest place for a lady to be walking alone. But I decided that a nice cold drink would be very pleasant, and I found a table. It was fun to watch the happy couples, the teenagers trying to look grown up, and the older people looking as if they were on holiday. As people began to eat, I became hungry and returned to my hotel for dinner.

In the morning, I ventured down the hill on Via Veneto to explore the shops. I bought some lovely soft white kid leather gloves. But I did not go too far, as Bill was to pick me up at twelve for lunch and some sightseeing. I smiled to myself as I got back to the hotel and saw a bellboy paging me with my name on a cardboard sign. What a clever way for him to find me.

The traffic was horrendous, but Bill and I arrived at a small, quiet sidewalk café safely. I always like to try local food, so we started with an Italian drink, a Compari, then melon wrapped in a thin slice of prosciuto ham (different, but delicious), a pasta dish, and ended with Italian ice cream. We had a wonderful time, talking non-stop during lunch and all through the tour of the city.

Bill was interested in what we had done in Vancouver for his pet project in Mysore, India: an educational institute built in Mysore to teach people how to preserve food. He took me to the F.A.O. building to meet the man in charge of the project. It was fascinating and inspiring. People were being brought into Mysore for six weeks, six months, or one year, depending on the requirements. Village leaders were brought in to teach their people how to preserve fruit and vegetables, and how to rodent-proof containers that held their rice and other grains. Courses such as these were given to leaders from other countries such as Indonesia, and many other southern countries as well. I was so interested that I promised to go to Mysore and see the project in operation. They gave me a letter of introduction.

Bill then took me home via the famous Trevi Fountain. I threw 'three coins in the Fountain', and Bill sang that song for me. It was a lovely afternoon. This was my first visit to Rome, but it would not be my last. The next day, I caught the afternoon flight to Athens, Greece.

When I arrived at the airport in Athens, I was being paged. I had arranged for a tour agent to meet me, and he was there as I walked out of customs and immigration. He took care of my luggage, put me in a limousine, and told the driver to take me to the Hotel Grand Bretagne. Yes, they had a reservation for me, and yes, a bellboy would take my bags up for me if I could wait in the lobby for a few minutes. I sorted out my papers and checked my itinerary. I was booked at this hotel for only one night. The next day, I was to go by limousine to Vouliagemeni, a seaside resort, for two days rest. I had a lovely room in the Hotel Grand Bretagne, looking up one of the pretty tree-lined main streets. The only problem was traffic noise! There was a traffic light right under my window where the street ended; all the cars had to turn left or right where the main road went past the side of the hotel.

I decided to explore the area around the hotel. As I went out of the front door, I stood in surprise looking at the huge square block, called Constitution Square. At first I thought someone was holding a meeting. There were hundreds of chairs there, that all seemed to be facing one way, looking towards the main street. When I finally managed to cross the street, I could see that people were sitting in the chairs eating and drinking, and that food dispensers were all in a row at the front of the square. It was like a giant outdoor restaurant, and it was always busy. I decided to have a cup of coffee, and watch the people coming back into the city after going home for siesta.

I learned that there were four rush hours in Athens. One in the morning going to work, one going home at noon for siesta, one when returning to the city around four or five o'clock, and, the last, returning home between seven or eight in the evening. Most of the stores and offices were closed tight during siesta. Although many cafés were closed, also, Constitution Square was always open. Early evening was a fascinating sight there. Stores were turning on their lights, office buildings lighting up, and airline and tourist counters doing a rushing business.

I was lucky to be at the King's Palace, which was just across the street, when there was a changing of the guards. The guards marched and changed places and rifles very smartly. Their military attire was vastly different from our uniforms. It was a colourful sight, and the end of a wonderful day, and I felt as if I was falling in love with Greece. One more walk around Constitution Square, then it was time for dinner, and then to my room. I was leaving for the holiday resort in the morning, and I needed to repack my bags. The hotel would keep my bigger bags until my return, when I would stay for three more nights.

The promised limousine arrived promptly at ten the next morning, and took me through the lovely countryside to the small village of Vouliagemeni, which had a small beach, and a large white marble hotel, the Astir Palace Hotel. My beautiful room looked out over the pretty little bay and the blue Aegean Sea. It was luxurious and restful. I was relieved to only have to wonder where I would find the lunch room. Much to my delight, the lunch room looked out over the bay and I could see people swimming. The idea of a swim in that calm sea on this hot day was appealing.

The hotel was not right on the beach, but had a large wharf and float with steps leading into the deep water. There were many people swimming, but not one splashing lap swimmer. Heads were moving along seemingly without any effort in the salt water. It was one of those special times to remember—the balmy sea, blue sky, and my white marble palace waiting for me peacefully in the late afternoon sun. When a swimmer came out of the water, an attendant had a large beach towel ready to wrap around the swimmer. I am sure the bathroom was designed with swimmers in mind. The shower alcove had a seat and water shooting out at all levels, making it easy to wash off the salt water and sand from their feet.

On my final evening, I ate a leisurely dinner looking out over this lovely restful, sunset scene. I felt as if I had been there for a week. After a good nights sleep, I felt relaxed and ready for the next lap of my journey. My faithful limousine and driver arrived just after lunch. As we were returning to the Hotel Grand Bretagne in the post-siesta rush, stopping in front of the hotel was hazardous. The driver practically dumped me out on the sidewalk, and the doorman rescued my bag, and me. But it was quiet and peaceful inside. The hotel had a room reserved for me and the luggage I had left behind was already in my room.

I relaxed on the bed and decided not to tackle the rush hour traffic. Realizing that I would be here for three nights, I hung up a few clothes, and then checked my Athens itinerary. There was to be a bus trip to the Acropolis the next morning, followed, the next day, by an all day trip south across the Corinthian Canal. That evening, I walked around Constitution Square and reconfirmed my plane reservations for the next leg of my trip, to Istanbul, Ankara, and Beirut. The Pan American Airline ticket office was on the other side of the Square, but by this time the crowds had thinned out, and it was a pleasant walk, looking at the shops that were now open.

At ten the next morning, I was waiting for the tour bus at the side door of the hotel. The bus was late, and I began to wonder if I had made a mistake. I glanced at the other person who seemed to be waiting for the tour bus, too. He was a young man with red hair, blue eyes and fair skin. Assuming that he was British and could speak English, I asked him if he was waiting for the tour bus. He was, and he reassured me. The bus was just late, he said. Many Greek people were notorious for being casual about time, sometimes being as much as an hour late for a party. Then he politely introduced himself as Nigel Gentner. After introducing myself, I asked him if he was British.

"No, I am Norwegian," he said, "but I went to school in England and graduated from Cambridge. I'm now married and living in

Paris." He explained that he was on his way to East Africa, and would be catching a six a.m. flight the next day.

The bus arrived, and we were able to get seats together. He told me he worked with the United Nations, specializing in urban development. I mentioned that I had lunched with Bill Gall, who was with F.A.O. He asked me what I was doing in Athens, and laughed heartily at my answer. "You, my dear lady, you expect me to believe that you are going to Vancouver from Rome via Athens, Turkey, Lebanon, Iran, India, Thailand, Hong Kong, Japan and Honolulu?" I laughed, and explained that I had been going to visit friends in Iran, the Friesens, and that it cost only seventy-five dollars more to go the rest of the way around the world.

The bus parked, and we walked up to the Parthenon at the top of the Acropolis. He had been there before, so he was able to give me a private guided tour, explaining about it being a temple of worship to the gods. In ancient times the city developed around the Acropolis. When the marketplace, or agora, became the place to meet, the city spread out on the plain. When the bus took us to the agora we could see how dramatically the market place had become a commercial centre, and the meeting place had moved to the government buildings.

When our bus arrived back at the hotel, Nigel invited me to have dinner with him on the roof garden of his hotel, just next door. We could eat dinner and watch the 'Symphony of Lights' which lit up the Acropolis with changing colours. We would not be able to hear the music, but the lighting effects would be spectacular. I agreed, and he said that he would call for me at seven-thirty.

In the afternoon, I walked around the city centre, but found that it was siesta time, and that nothing was open. There was a tiny church in a small square, but when I tried the door, it was locked, too. Finally I gave up and joined the siesta habit. I had a rest before dressing for dinner with my new friend.

It was a delightful evening. We had a table with an interesting view. Below us was the busy Constitution Square, to the left was the Palace with the guards standing stiff and still, across the square the airline offices and the stores were still open, and to our right, the Acropolis! As it grew dark, the lights came on. The different colours came and went, leaving us fascinated. The most spectacular combination was the time when all lights were turned off, then just the top of the Acropolis was a blaze of white and soft-blue lights, giving it a look as if it was floating in the air going up to heaven! We talked continuously and I enjoyed every minute. But it was time to go home, and Nigel escorted me back to my hotel. He gave me his card and asked me to let him know if I should go to Paris; he and his wife would show me Paris as few tourists ever see it.

The next morning I felt as if I had had a wee bit too much to drink the night before. But I soon felt better, and, as the tour to Corinth was not until noon, I walked over to see the Hilton Hotel, and ordered a mousaka for lunch.

The tour began by taking us eastward to the port of Piraeus, where all the famous Greek Island ships drop off their passengers. It was a small but very busy port. The drive through the countryside was lovely. When we stopped at the Corinthian Canal, I was astonished to see how deep they had made the cut, and how small the ships looked in it. At the beginning of the century, and without power tools, these amazing Greeks had carved out a water route from the inlet on the Adriatic to the Aegean Sea, making the sea route from the east coast to the west coast more than a hundred miles shorter. After crossing over the canal, the country seemed drier, the villages poorer, and the landscape less mountainous. We had dinner at a famous restaurant on the top of a promontory overlooking a beautiful bay.

In a valley, on our return trip, we visited one of the famous old amphitheatres where many ancient Greek tragic plays were performed. Then we crossed back over the Corinthian Canal, and drove through the pretty countryside to the hotel. It was dark when we arrived back. I packed my bags, ready for the next adventure—Istanbul!

Detail of the tile designs of the Blue mosque in Isfahan, Iran.

The gateway to the Taj Mahal, more colourful than the white Taj Mahal, Agra, India.

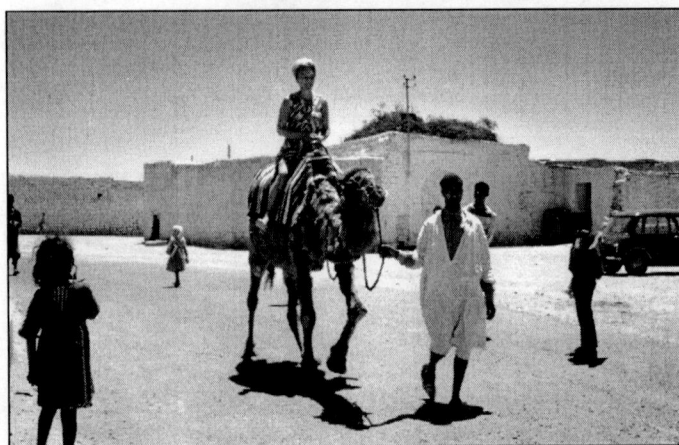

Anne riding gracefully on the camel in Tunisia.

TURKEY AND LEBANON

I was slightly nervous on my flight to Istanbul the next morning. I had seen many pictures of dark alleys and international intrigue, and I had a warped idea of this ancient city. As I waited in line at the customs and immigration counter in Istanbul, I heard some-one being paged. I finally realized that funny name was supposed to be mine. Would I please report to the Pan American courtesy counter, the voice said. The young woman at the counter spoke English well, and explained that the gentleman with the Hilton Hotel car would take me to my hotel. He took my bags, pushed through the airport confusion to a taxi stand, and drove to the Hilton Hotel. I was certainly glad that I had someone to guide me. It was a relief to step into the well organized Hilton institution. In foreign countries when travelling alone, I like to stay at a Hilton Hotel. There are always some employees who speak English.

"Yes, madam, we have a nice room overlooking the Bosporus reserved just for you." It was a lovely room with a beautiful view. It was nice to flop down on the bed for five minutes.

Then it was lunch time. I found the coffee shop, and was lucky to get a table by the window with a different view of the Bosporus. After lunch I sat out on the cool terrace drinking 'Turkish' coffee and enjoying the spectacular view. I decided to go for a ride on the ferry across the Bosporous going from Europe to Asia.

I started to walk to the city, but it was very hot, so I caught a taxi. When my taxi got near the ferry landing, with the confusion of hundreds of people milling around, some rushing to catch the departing ferry, and others pushing off a ferry, I decided that it was too much for me, and ordered the taxi to take me back to the hotel. The traffic to and from the hotel was wild; there did not seem to be any rules. Cars were parked on sidewalks; cars passed on sidewalks. When I arrived back at the hotel, the doorman helped me pay the taxi driver. He was talking loudly, and I could not understand a word. I had not changed my money at the airport, as I usually do, but the Hilton was always willing to exchange my traveller's cheques for local money. After an early dinner, I was out on the terrace with a Turkish coffee, checking my tour vouchers for my trip to explore the city of Istanbul.

The sightseeing bus was waiting at the door for me at ten the next morning. When I took my favourite front seat, I noticed that a fair haired man about thirty years old was sitting in the opposite seat, and that he had a small Rollei camera, just like the new one I had bought for the trip. We drove under a massive Roman aqueduct, and everyone got out to take a picture. As we were getting back into the bus, I asked him if he spoke English. As he said yes, I asked him how he liked his Rollei camera. "Well, I do not know yet. I only bought it yesterday in Sofia." I was curious and asked him why he would buy a camera in Sofia. He explained that he was a language professor and had been in Bulgaria without a camera, saw this small one, and bought it.

We walked into the Haggia Sophia Mosque, listening to the guide who was telling us about how it was built in 437 AD. Later, the

Mosque was turned into a Christian Church for a hundred years, then converted back into a mosque, with all of the Christian paintings covered with plaster and tiles.

As we went back to the bus, Ted, my new friend, asked me where I lived. When I said Vancouver, Canada, he laughed and told me that he lived in Vancouver, too! He asked me what I was doing in Istanbul. When I told him about the Moorish World trip, he laughed again, in obvious astonishment, and asked me if I had been at the first lecture about Spain at the University of British Columbia, when the projector broke down. I said that I had been there with my friend, Marta Friesen, who I was on my way to visit in Iran. We both stopped and stood amazed when he told me that he was the one running the projector! Later over lunch we marveled at the fact that we were both sitting here from Vancouver looking at the marvelous view from a little restaurant. We were watching the ferries going back and forth between Europe and Asia.

On our left was the Golden Horn, where the ferries leave to cross the Sea of Marmara to the Asian part of Istanbul, where the Florence Nightingale Hospital stands at the top of the hill. The Sea of Marmara narrows into the Bosporus, where ocean-going ships sail up to the Black Sea and Russian ports. Two large ships were passing each other as we watched. One going east to the Bosporus, and the other west through the Sea of Marmara and the Dardanelles to the Aegean. It was an impressive view of this historic city.

Ted was good company, but we had to join the tour to see the various aspects of the ancient Seraglio. There were whole wings of this enormous Sultan's palace where the women of the harem lived. There, no man could enter except the eunuchs (a neutered male servant). There were so many wings that I wondered if people got lost. The kitchen was a large room with six or seven huge stoves and hundreds of different sets of dishes. Finally we came to the jewel room. There were jewels set in all kinds of objects, as well as gorgeous jewelry for ladies. After this, the tour ended and we were driven back to our hotels. I was going to dinner with friends that evening, and then to Ankara next day. Ted and I said our farewells.

My plans changed. My friends, the Toros—whom I had met in South America at the conference of the Experiment in International Living -had urged me to take a Bosporus cruise to the Black Sea, and I arranged with the hotel to do it the next morning. It was a lovely day, and I was able to get a seat on the top deck. When I looked up from my tour pamphlet, I was astonished to see my friend Ted walking towards me. When he caught sight of me, we both laughed. "This cannot be true. Where did you come from?" I moved over, and he sat down beside me shaking his head in dis-belief! "You did not mention that you were coming on the cruise. I thought that you were going to Ankara?" I explained about my change of plans.

As we passed palaces and estates with wharves, we realized that in past decades water transportation had been very important. We came up to the Romeli Fort, which was not used any more as a fort, but as a place for concerts. The fort had been built on a narrow spot in the Bosporus. Then it widened again, and ships turned there, to return to Istanbul, and beyond. Beyond this turning-point were Communist Russian fortifications. We docked at a waterside café, and all enjoyed a leisurely lunch watching ships and yachts manoeuvring for the return trip. A Russian warship sailed through peacefully, bound for the Sea of Marmara, the Dardanelles, and the Aegean Sea. The fortifications were impressive on both sides of the narrow opening to the Russian-controlled Black Sea. I was disap-pointed that we could not go any further, but it was a lovely trip, and it was so nice to share it with Ted.

On the way back to Istanbul, Ted asked me if I would have dinner with him at the Hilton roof-top dining room. I thought it was a wonderful idea. We met in the lobby of my hotel, and went up to the dining room. During dinner, I told him about my evening with the Toros family.

The son of my friend Meliha had picked me up and driven me to their house. It was a very funny evening. Meliha excused herself, asking her husband to look after me while she checked on how her new cook was doing with dinner. Mr. Toros was very gallant, but found it difficult to converse with me as his English was even poorer than my French! He ushered me out to a comfortable chair on the balcony where the view was beautiful, overlooking the Bosporus and to the west, the Sea of Marmara. I could understand that he was offering me a drink of raki, the Turkish specialty. As he poured it, he explained that if you added water the drink would turn milky.

I finally understood that he was in the government department of trade and commerce, and that his particular interest was in buying lumber. Not from British Columbia, he said, but from Sweden. I tried to get him to consider buying lumber from us, but my French was not up to his and he did not understand me. We did better when he talked about Turkish history. He told me how Ataturk was the hero who had joined the various parts of the country together, and made Ankara the capital.

Eventually Meliha rescued us by calling us in to dinner. Their son joined us, and as his English was good, the conversation was in English, with Meliha telling her husband what we were saying. They all decided that I must put off my reservation for Ankara and go on the boat trip to the Black Sea and that on the morning after that, Meliha would take me to the covered bazaar.

Ted and I had a table by the window overlooking the gorgeous view. The speciality of the day was an unusual lamb dish. Slices of lamb were put on an upright skewer around and around to the top and then revolved past a flaming panel. When an order was asked for, the spit was stopped and the outside browned meat was carved off and put on the hot plate. These delicately browned and sizzled pieces of lamb were superb—the best lamb that I have ever tasted.

We talked about the cruise, speculated about Russian warships using the Bosporus, the Sea of Marmara, and the Dardanelles to reach the Aegean Sea. There was so much to see and learn about this fascinating country. We watched the sunset and the lights of the Asian and European side of the city shining bright below us. After our last cup of Turkish black coffee, we parted, agreeing to meet again in Vancouver. He was returning to Sofia and I would soon be on my way to Ankara.

Meliha called for me to guide me through the covered bazaar, which spread out over a huge area. The stalls, or booths, sold everything movable. Food of all kinds, jewelry, stationery, pots and pans, clothes, brass things, drugs, cosmetics, shoes, hats, lumber, and many other items. It was nice having Meliha to fend off the pushy salesmen, and advise me on what was or was not a bargain. My only purchase was a tiny ring, which Meliha explained was a harem ring—really five small rings fastened together, each one with a small turquoise set in the middle. The harem rings would signify whether you were number one wife, with only one ring, or, as mine had five rings, it meant that I was wife number five.

We ended the morning tour by taking the ferry to the other side of Istanbul, to the Asian area, where the Florence Nightingale Hospital still stands. We were told the story of Florence Nightingale, how she was one of the most important persons in the history of nursing. Although she had very little training as a nurse, she volunteered to go to rescue the soldiers in the Crimean War. She and her heroic helpers were not prepared for the horrendous slaughter of the British soldiers. With practically no equipment and few doctors she struggled to save lives as soldiers lay bleeding to death. She trained local women to help wherever they could. When the war was over, she returned to England, and immediately pushed the authorities to start a training program for nurses. Through her efforts, the London hospitals began training programs. Soon nursing became a profession, with standards which were recognized all over the world.

Late that afternoon, I flew to Ankara. Meliha had written the name of the Ankara hotel on an envelope for me to give to the taxi driver in case he could not understand my English. When we arrived at the hotel, I was sure that it was not the right one, but the name was the same as the one on my envelope. It was a small hotel with an unkempt garden and badly in need of paint. Unfortunately, I had paid the taxi fare and it had disappeared. I had no choice but had to carry my bags into this sad looking hotel.

The room that they took me to was just as unkempt. The room was "our best, in the front, with its own private bathroom", the clerk said, in broken English, as he carried my bags up the staircase and opened the door for me. As it was getting dark, I did not have the courage to try to find a better hotel. When I went into the dark bathroom to wash up for dinner, it was equally depressing. But I was hungry, and found that the hot water was hot. Feeling slightly refreshed, I found my way to the dining room. The menu was in Turkish, and nobody seemed to understand me, but I ordered a meat dish that was quite good, and some nice fresh bread.

Back in my room, I decided to go to bed and change hotels in the morning. All hotels are supposed to post their rates in an available spot, usually on the back of a closet door. When I found this document, the declared rate was about five dollars per night. I had been charged thirty dollars for the night in my prepaid reservation! I was going to go to the head of the tourist bureau and demand a refund! With this in mind, I decided to take a shower and rally forth in the morning. When I turned on the water, it sprayed the whole room, including my dressing gown, and the water drained down a central drain, out of which came a horrible smell; obviously also the drain for the toilet. Ugh. I began to laugh. What a contrast from the previous nights at the Hilton in Istanbul. The bed was rumpled as if it had just been slept in, so I slept on the top of the bedspread. I was becoming a seasoned traveller.

In the morning I checked out, and decided to go to the Pan

American airline ticket office about my reservations on the flight to Beirut, Lebanon, the next day. Then I would look for a new hotel. The young woman in the ticket office spoke English. When I showed her my ticket, she exclaimed, shaking her head, "But, my dear lady, we do not have a flight to Lebanon that day." I said, "Well, what am I going to do? I have reservations to continue on to Iran." She replied, " Why don't you wait until the manager comes back from his coffee break? He might be able to get you on another flight." I thanked her and sat down to wait. When he came in he invited me into his office.

His secretary explained the problem, and he said that he would see what he could do about getting me on another flight. "Could I see your ticket, please, and your passport?" When he saw my passport, he exclaimed, "Ah, a Canadian! My wife is Canadian." At my questioning look, he told me that he had been posted to Canada for six years. We talked about Canada, and the French problem; he and his wife had lived in Montreal for four years, representing Pan American Airlines. He suggested that I should leave my passport and ticket with him, and that he would see what he could do for me. I asked about a hotel for the night, and he suggested that the hotel across the street was very nice—"we put all of our crews, there." He had his secretary call the hotel to make a reservation and then had a boy take my bags over for me.

After lunch, I took a tour to see the sights of Ankara. The Ataturk Mausoleum was a surprise to me because of its size and impressive situation. The huge plaza in front of the actual vault was in line with four lions at each corner, and statues of all kinds of workmen. The tomb was in the middle of the vault, with a carving of Ataturk lying as if asleep on top of the coffin.

Ataturk was a remarkable man who accomplished almost impossible tasks. To unify the country, roads and railways had to be built through deserts. Telephone and telegraph lines had to be stretched from one end of the country to the other. The absolute power of the

Sultans and Moslem leaders had to be abolished. The Greeks were finally forced out of their last stronghold around Izmir, about 1928. A new language was created using the English, French, and German words and alphabets. Ataturk's aim was to have a unified and democratic country, Turkey. As I left the tomb and looked down over the city, I felt full of awe thinking of this man. Ataturk— the man who had the audacity and the courage to dream such dreams and the persuasive power to have others share his dreams and work to make these dreams come true. As I turned to go, I took pictures of the city and the pretty countryside.

Back at the hotel, I found a message asking me to go to the Pan Am Airline office. I was welcomed with smiles and invited into the manager's office. "We have managed to get you on another airline that leaves at two tomorrow. We have notified our Beirut office that you will arrive one hour earlier, and they will be sending someone to meet you and take you to your hotel. I hope you have a happy visit with your friends in Iran."

He gave me my amended ticket and passport and stood up to shake hands with me, and said with a smile, "By the way, a car will be calling for you to take you to the airport at twelve noon." I went back to the hotel smiling and happy with the solution of my problem, and the warm friendly help from this kind stranger.

The 'car' waiting for me at noon turned out to be a Rolls Royce limousine with an uniformed chauffeur who could not speak English. I never did find out who owned the car. When I got to the airport and checked in at the ticket counter, the attendant took my ticket and gave me my boarding pass, saying, "We are expecting you. The plane will be twenty minutes late, so this young lady will take you to a comfortable lounge where you can wait until the flight is called. I hope you have a pleasant flight." I followed the young lady, and realized that I was being given the VIP treatment, and when I finally boarded the plane, I was taken to a reserved seat. When I looked questioningly at her, she nodded and said in French,

"Yes, for you."

After we had gained altitude, the other stewardess came and asked me if I would like to visit the cockpit? When the stewardess introduced me to the pilot and co-pilot, they closed the door and offered me a jump seat to sit on and started pointing out cities and towns about 32,000 feet below us. Although they told me they were both Lebanese, they spoke excellent English. This surprised me. They explained that all airline pilots had to be able to speak English, as well as all air traffic controllers, in order to bring planes in for a safe landing. We talked about airports in other countries and then they asked me why I was in this part of the world. I explained about the Moorish World tour, and they insisted that the Phoenicians and the sailors from Lebanon were masters of the Mediterranean, even before the Romans. As we flew over the Mediterranean, we marveled at the courage of those ancient sailors.

The island of Cypress was below us, looking dry and desolate. We wondered aloud why the Greeks and the Turkish people would fight over such an island. Now, as they were preparing for a landing, I had to return to my seat. It had been a fascinating few hours.

As I finished with customs and immigration, I thought my name was coming over the loud speaker. I was right. A young man was holding up a sign with my name on it. When I identified myself, the handsome young man explained that the Pan Am office had been asked to look after me for twenty-four hours, and take me to the airport to catch the Pan Am flight to Iran. My new guide was very helpful and friendly, and spoke very good English. We drove the scenic route to the Phoenician Hotel, a large modern pink building overlooking the Mediterranean. My new friend helped me check into the hotel, and said that he would pick me up at nine the next morning, to show me 'the most beautiful city in the world.'

I had dinner in the hotel dining room. I ordered the shish kebab by showing the waiter the Lebanese name for the lamb dish. I really did not need to worry about the language here, as most of the hotel employees did speak some English. After dinner I wandered around the hotel's little shops that were still open. One shop had the most beautiful silks. As I was looking at the gorgeous fabrics the salesman invited me in to see more. After some hesitation, I went in. He pulled many bolts of silk down and began draping them around me. I began to be nervous, feeling entangled. In the meantime, he kept on with his sales pitch about how his beautiful silks would make this pretty lady more beautiful. He would give me a good price, and on and on, saying, "I will take you out for dinner, and to my other shop, where I have more lovely silks and jewelry." I eased myself towards the door draping the samples of silks over his shoulders, entangling him in his own silks, and escaping out of the door.

I thought some fresh air would be a good idea, so I went out on the hotel terrace. I was on the low parapet, looking out at a small cove of the Mediterranean, when a young uniformed soldier sat down beside me. After a few pleasant remarks he invited me to have dinner with him. He was very insistent. Finally I told him that I was a grandmother and did not date strange men, and walked away to the hotel entrance. I was having quite a welcome to Beirut!

When I went to my room, I found it as cold as ice. I tried to turn down the air-conditioning, but nothing happened so I had a hot bath, pulled the extra cover from the other twin bed over me, and snuggled down for a good sleep. When I went down for breakfast, I asked if the temperature could be moderated, and they said, "No problem, we will send someone up to adjust the thermostat."

My young guide arrived at the hotel at nine to take me on my sight-seeing trip. The main shopping area seemed very glamorous, with jewelry and silk shops dominating the scene. Gold jewelry, earrings, bracelets, necklaces, and inlaid gold trinkets of all kinds filled the display counters. There was plenty of silverware, too. As we walked from jewelry store to silk shop, with a rug shop here and there, I marveled at the patience of this young man. I wondered if he would get a commission if his tourist passengers did buy anything. After our shopping expedition, we drove through the downtown area past modern office buildings and apartments. The residential area was very attractive, and overflowing with flowering shrubs and blossoming trees.

When we arrived at the shore of the Mediterranean, it looked very blue and enticing. I wished that I was going on a cruise instead of flying from country to country. The warehouse by the sea was huge and displayed rugs, all kinds of rugs! The salesman showed me beautiful rugs from India, Turkey, Iran, and Lebanon. He did his best to sell one to me, but I explained that I was travelling for many weeks and could not take a rug with me on the plane. "No problem, I can ship it to you." I declined his offer, thanked him for his rug display and left for my hotel, to have lunch and check out.

My kind guide was waiting for me in the limousine after lunch. We drove to the airport by another scenic route, where I said goodbye, thanking him for his kindness and patience. The Pan Am flight for Teheran, Iran, was called. I was looking forward to my next visit. My friends, Marta and John Friesen, would be meeting me at the airport, and I would be their guest for two weeks.

top left and right: The beautiful tiled mosques of Isfahan, Iran.

bottom: Girl weaving rugs in Tehran, Iran. The better rugs have hundreds of threads per inch.

The Golden Temple of Kinkakuji in Kyoto, Japan. Looking as if it was floating on the water.

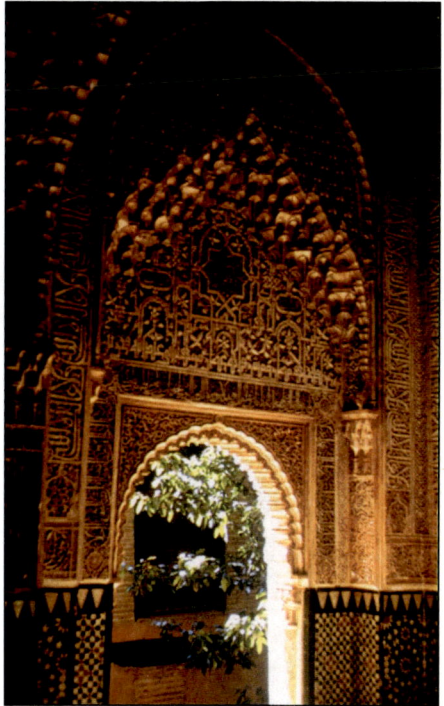

Inside the Alhambra, Granada, Spain. It is one of the most spectacular examples of Moorish architecture.

Marjory buying part of her Berber Costume in the market in Tunis, Tunisia. The Berbers were the colourful wild men of the mountains.

IRAN

We landed in Tehran, the capital of Iran. Marta and John Freisen were there to give me a wonderful warm welcome. It was like a happy homecoming. As we drove to their house everything seemed very dry and dusty. The high walled gardens lacked the softening effect of green shrubs and trees that had broken the harsh look of the residential area. At one end of one of these streets a gate opened and we drove into a different world. Although the garden was not very big, it was very pretty, with flowering shrubs, colourful flowers, and a blue tiled swimming pool.

The house was spacious and cool, built in the oriental style: square, with a flat roof. The front hall was spacious with colourful Turkish and Persian rugs scattered around and a white marble staircase. Each slab of marble looked as if it were suspended in space, but it actually was embedded in the solid wall and balanced by rods fastened to the floor above. The effect was pleasing to the eye, wonderfully cool, and smooth to the bare feet. The house had four bedrooms. I had a lovely room with my own bathroom. The view from my window was not very inspiring. All of the houses seemed to be built as if by piling blocks on top of each other. The flat roofs and high garden walls cut off my view of anything green. As the next day was Friday, a Moslem holy day, Marta and John offered to take me around Tehran.

In the morning, after a swim in their pool, they drove me to see the city centre. The office buildings were a mixture of the old and the new, with not many tall ones. They pointed out the government buildings, the banks, and the department stores. We drove by the bazaar, which was closed, quiet, and empty. The Moslems are very strict about observing the restrictions of their holy day. As we drove out of the city, the landscape became very dry and dusty. After we'd left the green irrigated farms behind us, the land became very dry, like a desert. About two thirds of the land is infertile. The extensive plans for irrigation projects were the only hope for the farmers. One of their biggest problems to solve was how to handle the nomads. These herdsmen migrated to the south of the land in the winter, then back north in the summer. They settled in a good grazing area until it was stripped. Then, with their tents, families, sheep, goats, camels, and other animals, the herdsmen moved to a fresh grazing area. Their ancestors were nomads for hundreds of years. They did not know any other way to make a living.

When we drove back to the city, we passed a huge rocky cliff where colourful rugs were spread out to dry. Evidently the water in this particular area had natural chemicals in it that would set the colours so they did not run or fade (hopefully). It was an interesting sight to see these women rinsing these valuable rugs, then spreading them in such a haphazard way on these rugged rocks. There were so many questions that I wanted to ask. How did they know which were theirs? How did they get the rugs to be flat, straight, and fluffy, like the ones I had seen in Beirut? Later on in the week we visited a rug factory and watched the women painstakingly making the beautiful rugs. The Iranians, formerly Persians, were the only Moslem country to decorate with flowers, trees, and leaves. The delicate Persian 'Miniatures' were a perfect example of tiny flowers and leaves being used for decorations.

Sunday was not a holy day in the Moslem world, so both Marta and John worked. I did not mind having a day to do some washing and sorting out my papers and traveller's cheques. When they came home that night they produced some pamphlets about sight-seeing tours, and we spent the evening discussing plans for my days in Iran. The next day would be spent seeing the museums, the Crown Jewels, and some of the government buildings. Then they suggested that I should fly to Isfahan and Shiraz. The Tehran museums were interesting, full of historic artifacts from the ancient Persian era. The Emerald Throne was spectacular, dazzling with emeralds, rubies, diamonds, and other precious jewels. The Crown Jewels were kept in the basement bank vault, as security for the value of the Iranian currency. After an eventful day, it was so wonderful to come home to have dinner with my beloved friends.

When I set off on the plane to Isfahan, I was loaded with brochures about the history of the former capital of Persia. Staying at the spectacular Shah Abas Hotel was an unforgettable experience. Some ingenious person had changed an old caravanserai into a fabulous hotel. In ancient times, when the caravans arrived, loaded with silks, jewels and spices, they needed somewhere safe to spend the night. These caravanserais were built like huge forts, in the form of a large square, with a large arched entrance in the front centre building. The caravans would go through the gate and the animals would be housed in the lower rooms, while the people would be looked after in the upper floors, safe from marauding bandits.

Now it was a beautiful hotel with all imaginable modern conveniences. The lobby was dazzling. The walls were finished in elaborate tile designs with shiny mirror inlays. Beautiful framed Persian miniatures were set in the plain spaces of the wall. I had a room on the second floor east wing overlooking the courtyard. It was a lovely room, and I liked looking out at the Moorish style garden, with its fountains and waterways connecting the numerous pools. It was hard to imagine that the lovely garden courtyard could have had dozens of camel trains, horses, carriages, and flocks of goats and sheep being bedded down for the night. It was very pleasant to sit out in the garden and be away from the tourist crowds.

I did go sightseeing, and was really astonished at the beauty of the Blue Mosque. The outside dome, completely covered with blue tile, was awe inspiring. And the inside was even more magnificent. The elaborate tile designs were incredible. Women are not allowed in the main part of the Mosque during religious services. Everyone had to take off their shoes before entering, and the men must kneel down and touch the floor with their foreheads during the prayers.

The minarets outside are used to call the worshipers to prayers. Now the calls are recorded, and the tape plays the calls instead of the Imam having to climb up to the top of the minaret, and call out loud. The minarets are tiled like the domes of the mosques, usually four of them, and the calls come from the north, south, east, and west. Once when I wandered into a mosque during prayer time, I was impressed with the kneeling figures—but also oppressed, because the women were herded back behind rope, like cattle, instead of being allowed to pray with their husbands and sons. I had wandered in by mistake, and was happy when I was back outside in the sunshine.

Isfahan was full of mosques. Another day, on a bus tour, I visited one, but it was not as big as the Blue Mosque. The tour guide took us into the country to see the Mountain of Fire. There were numerous paths and steps leading up to the top of the mountain where the Zoroaster worshipers would climb. I did not understand all that he said about Zoroasterism. As we drove by, many pilgrims were trudging up the steep trails towards the top. The bridges that crossed a river were more like Roman aqueducts, built with solid stone arches. Up the other side of the river, we came to an

Armenian Church in the Greek Orthodox style. It was an astounding contrast to the mosques that we had visited. The outside was just like many western churches, but the inside was the biggest surprise. Every inch of the walls were covered with Biblical scenes, statues and ornaments. How did this happen in this strictly Moslem country? The guide explained that the Armenian refugees built the church when Iran accepted hundreds of them who were fleeing from persecution in their homeland.

I spent some time admiring the beautiful work done by so many loving hands. The Nativity scene was so realistic that I expected the baby Jesus to wave His hands and the cows to moo. I wanted to go up to the altar and kneel down and pray for these brave people. Now, as I write these memories, I wonder what has happened to that dear little church. I have heard that my favourite hotel, the Shah Abas, has been demolished because it was too secular, so I do not think that the Armenian place of worship would have been spared after the Shah had been deposed.

After driving back across the river, we were taken to a playing field where there was a unique royal box, or viewing stand. The tile work was very elaborate, probably the most decorative viewing stand in the world. After driving by more mosques and some ancient buildings built when Isfahan was the capital city, we were returned to our hotel.

The next morning, I flew to Shiraz. The barren landscape below seemed to stretch endlessly. It was brown and rocky with green patches along a river. But Shiraz, itself, was surprisingly pretty, with wide boulevards. Down the centre of the divided main street was green grass with fragrant beds of roses. It was June and the roses were in full bloom, and it seemed like Shiraz was the City of Roses. The Summer Palace was lovely, and the pools and fountains gave the gardens a cool refreshing look. Across from the palace, there was a colourful garden with a plaque stating the belief that God is always present in a garden: "Welcome. God is nearer to you in a garden." There was a gate, and a plaque inviting me to go in and sit down on the little bench. I marveled at this gem of a garden, with its beautiful flowers surviving in the dry desert heat, and the loving care being taken. I wondered who would put up the unusual plaque, written in English?

There were more surprises. Someone had built two tombs for two of Iran's most famous poets, Hafiz and Saadi. The tombs were near each other, pretty, with well-kept gardens surrounding them. The actual tombs were in an enclosure of about ten by eight feet, decorated in the Persian style with inscriptions in flowing Arabic writing. After all the wonderful sights, I returned to the hotel very hot, and too tired for even a swim in the hotel pool.

There were no sightseeing tours to Persepolis while I was in Shiraz, so I hired a car and driver to take me to see one of the oldest of the Persian ruins, dating back to Darius the Second. Persepolis was constructed about six hundred B.C. After leaving the green landscape of Shiraz, the highway went through desolate country for about forty miles. On the way, I asked the driver to stop so that I could watch a tribe of nomads who were living in their black tents just a few miles from the highway. Off in the distance, I could see their herds of goats, sheep, and some camels. With all of those animals eating every slip of greenery, wandering across the country, they would leave that area barren, then move on to new greener pastures. I wondered if the nomads caused the deserts, or did they become nomads to survive?

There were not many people living at Persepolis in 1969, but the ruins were impressive. The massive flat surface with some of the columns still standing gave an impression of astonishing grandeur for so ancient a civilization. To me, the most memorable part was the frieze between the two sets of steps. The carvings were remarkably real and well preserved, having been buried in the sand for hundreds of years. The soldiers in their armour and helmets were very life-like, and the horses seemed to be holding their legs as if ready for battle. The carvings, about one hundred feet wide and ten feet high, covered the whole wall at the north entrance. The intense heat finally forced me back to the car, and the drive back to Shiraz seemed longer than forty miles. As I had walked around and over the ruins for several hours, my air-conditioned room was a most welcome sight.

As I flew out of Shiraz next morning I looked in all directions to see if the famous oil fields were visible in the direction of the Persian Gulf. Petroleum was Iran's most important export. However, I was not able to see any signs of oil production. But I did see where the Iranians had built dams, and the results of the irrigation systems.

Marta met me at the airport and drove me around the city and to a fruit market on the way home. We went for a swim in their pleasant little swimming pool. I settled in again in my lovely little room. For dinner that night, Marta served a variety of delicious tropical and semi-tropical fruits. The peaches, persimmons, and Persian melons were delicious. We had bought them at the market on our way home, and had been told that the fruit came from the Caspian Sea area. Because the Caspian Sea was below sea level and the land at the south end of the sea was very fertile, they could grow an immense variety of tropical and semi-tropical fruit and vegetables. It seemed strange to me that they went north for tropical climate and vegetation.

Most of Iran is on a high plateau. Tehran is cut off from the Caspian Sea by a long ridge of mountains to the north. The sea is a great asset for Iran because of the prosperous fishing industry, as well as the other obvious advantages. I wished that I had had time to visit the Caspian Sea area.

The next day Marta dropped me off in the city centre where I went shopping, spending a long time in the department stores finding something to buy. After browsing for over an hour, I decided to buy a pair of socks. It was hilarious, the clerk and me trying to make each other understood. We finally used our hands and fingers, coming up with an agreeable figure. I gave her the correct change, and carried my purchase away as if I had won first prize!

I went to the nearest hotel and asked the doorman if he could get a taxi for me. I also asked if he could direct the taxi driver to the Freisens' address, that John had printed out for me earlier. Between the two of them they decided where to go, and I was happy to arrive home, paying the cab driver the amount on the meter.

As I had been included in an invitation to a very special dinner party that night, I decided to have a rest before getting dressed up. When Marta and John came home they had a short swim, then joined me for a short cocktail. Our hosts would not be serving drinks because of their religious beliefs. John explained that our host and hostess were both from India, and that they were entertaining some important official connected with the consulate.

When we arrived, we were ushered into a spacious entrance hall, then taken into the reception room, where we were formally introduced to the special guests in the receiving line. The dinner was an elaborate buffet. Several rooms were set with different courses. I had a wonderful time after the formalities were over. I was free to wander around admiring the elaborate display of unusual looking food. I went from one room to the other sampling delicacies, all vegetarian. There must have been over a hundred different dishes. I would take a plate in the first room, a try a little of this and a little of that. Sometimes I would be introduced to a guest who could speak English. We would chat for a while, then I would move on to the next room, sampling different dishes there—until there were no other rooms. John and Marta would catch up with me and introduce me to more people. It was great fun.

When I was not busy eating, I would watch the fascinating people. The most memorable ladies were the ones from India. The elaborate and dramatic sari costumes dominated the scene, creating a colourful background for the sparkling jewels glittering around their necks, wrists, and ears and in their hair. We Westerners looked drab and ordinary among such beautiful ladies. Marta introduced me to one of these gorgeous guests. I was very surprised when she asked me to be her guest at one of her dinner parties when I was in India the next week. I was very pleased to be invited to her home, and knew that it would minimize my loneliness in the strange city of New Delhi. When we were leaving, my new friend came to say goodbye. "Here is my address, but you do not need to worry, as we will send a car to pick you up at your hotel, the Intercontinental, at seven p.m. on the Thursday." I thanked her, and followed Marta and John to their car.

On the way home, Marta told me about my new friend, Laura Lambert. Marta and John had met Laura and her husband, Derek, in Jaipur, and had become good friends. I asked about their nationality, "If they are both native born East Indians, how did they have English names?" John explained that long ago, Christians were persuaded to take English names, but other religious sects could not do so. Generations ago, Derek's family chose Lambert, and when he married Laura, she became Laura Lee Lambert. "By the way, they are interested in the Experiment in International Living, and have had groups in their home in New Delhi."

Since 1965, I, too, had been involved in the Experiment in International Living (EIL). Through EIL, we had a young Mexican stay in our home as a member of our family. I had been asked to represent Canada; Canada was petitioning to be accepted as a member of this organization. And I kept in touch with the friends I had met at this conference.

The next morning, being my last day, Marta took me shopping. Our first visit was to the covered Bazaar. We bought some useful items, and then it was time to explore the fabulous jewelry booths. Marta knew of one that was reputed to be honest. As Iran was famous for turquoise jewelry, I was determined to buy something to remind me of Marta and John's hospitality. I finally settled on a beautiful necklace, which was surprisingly reasonable. I fell in love with it and have treasured it for years. It was exquisitely made to look like a cluster of grapes. There were seven clusters of turquoise nestled in mock gold leaves. I bought a brooch for Marta and pair of cufflinks for John. We had lunch in the little restaurant, then returned home and had a swim before I went up to pack. Marta and John insisted that they would drive me to the airport that evening.

After a special farewell dinner, we talked about India, which was my next stop, about Iran, and how much I had been able to see, and what I should have seen. As usual there is never enough time to do all the visiting that one would like to do. We talked until the last minute and the flight was called.

The plane was almost full, so I had to settle for an aisle seat. After the routine of the take-off announcement, and the passing out of blankets and pillows, I tried to get comfortable for some sleep. It was now nearly two a.m., and we were not due to arrive in New Delhi until five. I did want some sleep, but when they passed out the earphones for a movie, I gave up and paid two dollars and fifty cents to hear the sound. It was in colour on a big screen, so I plugged in the earphones, pushed some buttons and heard talking, but I could not understand one word! Scenes were changing, people going in and out of Paris hotel rooms, men playing cards, pretty girls flirting, but, in spite of changing dials and pushing buttons, I could not understand a word. Suddenly I realised that I was on an Air France plane, and, of course, the film would be in French!

Persian ruins of Darius II. Persepolis was the
capital of Persia, now called Iran.
The carved warriors looked fierce enough
to keep me from climbing the stairs.

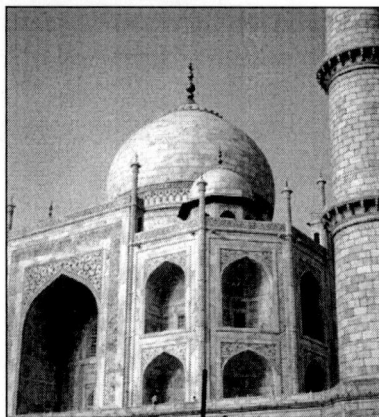

At Agra, India, a section of
the Taj Mahal. One of the
most beautiful of the Seven
Wonders of the World.

Marjory admiring one of
the statues near the Imperial
Palace in Bangkok Thailand.

INDIA and THAILAND

My arrival in New Delhi was one long series of confusing events. The customs official was very stuffy, insisting on pulling out practically everything, even my dirty clothes bag. Then he pushed my bag down the counter for me to attempt to put everything back into my two suitcases. It was hot and I was tired. Finally, with the help of some of the other passengers, I shut the bags, passed through immigration—and into bedlam! It seemed that fifteen boys were dead set on carrying my bags to the taxi stand. But, for the first time in my life, I was determined to carry my own bags.

As I passed out the door to the taxi stand, six more pairs of hands grabbed at my bags. I picked out the nearest cab pushed my bags into the front seat, climbed into the back seat and shut the door! When ONE of the pairs of hands took hold of the wheel, I sighed with relief. "Can you take me to the Oberoi Intercontinental Hotel, please?" "Yes, Memsahib, I can do that for you," was the welcome answer.

The ride to the hotel was interesting. It was beginning to get light, and I could see houses and trees. The roads at that time of day were almost empty, except for the wandering cows, and a few bicyclers. The Intercontinental Hotel was used to travellers arriving at unusual hours. I had the taxi driver carry my bags into the hotel and wait for me to cash a traveller's cheque so that I could pay him. In the confusion at the airport, I had not purchased any local currency.

My room was ready. The bellboy took my bags up for me and the male maid turned down my bed and brought me clean towels for the bathroom. I never got used to men attending me in the bedroom. After the maid had left, I washed, undressed, climbed into bed and slept for three hours.

The sun was high in the sky when I woke up. I felt like it was a new day. I phoned down to the desk to get the correct India time. It was quarter to eleven in the morning. Because of the mess that the customs man had made in my luggage, I reorganized everything, put on a fresh summer dress and went out to explore this lovely hotel and plan my sightseeing tours. I had vouchers for a tour to the Taj Mahal and the famous Red Fort. After lunch, I planned to see the Parliament Buildings and the city centre.

The Parliament Buildings were unusual. The architecture was more European with a touch of the Oriental in the decorative, reddish brick trimming. New Delhi had taken over as the official city in about 1939, but Old Delhi was still part of the business centre. This unusual arrangement gave New Delhi a look of a city without a centre.

It took some courage to go through the crowded market, but I marveled at the endless variety of familiar and unfamiliar fruits and vegetables. I was particularly interested in the beautiful inlaid brass work. There were three legged stools, bowls of every size and shape, urns, water jugs, trays, and dainty jewelry displayed in one shop. I had a wonderful time admiring the lovely things. The sales-man spoke English very well and explained how the inlay designs were hammered into the brass over heat. He took me to watch the artisans beating the colours into the designs on the brass. I was fas-cinated. What wonderful gifts they would make! The salesman suggested that he could pack and ship anything to any place in the world. The prices were very reasonable, and I was hooked. I explained that I would think it over, and that if I decided to buy, I would be back in two days with names and addresses.

One of the novelties in the area was the shoeshine boys. They had little stands like tool boxes with a place to put a foot so the boy could shine a person's shoe. They were everywhere, and could be very insistent. One small boy kept pestering me. I had stopped at a light to cross the street when I felt a slight push and a splash. The shoeshine brat was laughing and running away. I looked down at my foot and saw a great splash of black shoe polish across my white shoes! The light changed and I had to cross the street. What was I going to do? I looked up and saw that the Air India ticket office occupied the corner store front; maybe someone there could help me.

The kind employee pulled out a chair for me, bringing paper tow-els to wipe off the black blob of shoe polish. They had a washroom and produced a wet cloth and a towel to wash and dry my feet. One of the ladies suggested that I could take my shoes to the cobbler to have them cleaned and whitened professionally. The cobbler was very near, and did a good job. I went back to the ticket office and thanked them for their kindness. They called a taxi for me. I was hot and tired, and I was very glad to be going back to my air-condi-tioned hotel.

At dinner, I tried a chicken curry dish that was listed as mild. The curry was so hot that I grabbed a bun and tried to cool down my throat, and wash away the burning sensation by drinking great gulps of water. Nothing helped! I accused the waiter of mixing my order, but he declared that I had what I had ordered, pointing to the name of the dish that I had asked for. When I looked at the menu: chicken was the hot dish! I am very fond of curried foods and have eaten curried chicken and curried shrimp innumerable times, but never any so hot! I had looked forward to eating curry in India. Happily, I did have many mild curry dishes there that were delicious.

When I finished my dinner, I wandered through the hotel boutique shops. I visited several of them, but found three of them most interesting. The man in the jewelry shop spoke excellent English. He assured me that most of his jewels were found in India. He persuaded me to look at some real jewels, not set, that I could buy reasonably. The jewels could be taken home to be made into rings, bracelets, or necklaces. I had a wonderful time looking at rubies, emeralds, sapphires, and diamonds! It was an unusual happening. He was obviously enjoying his beautiful collection, and was not pressuring me. I finally did buy an alexandrite, about the size of my middle finger nail. It was so beautiful. The different shades of wine red, purple and blue were fascinating. Years later, my husband had it made into a ring for my birthday.

My next visit was to the brass shop. I was very excited. The wonderful brass things, which I had seen in the big bazaar, were here in my hotel! I decided that this place would be more reliable for buying and shipping things home. It was getting late, and I made arrangements to give the salesman names and addresses on the Thursday morning. As I was leaving for the Taj Mahal at six the next morning, I made a short list of people and gifts, and went to bed early, leaving a message at the desk to call me at 5 a.m.

At such times as this, I was very grateful for modern first class hotels where employees are trained to aid guests in any emergency. The desk clerk had a taxi for me in minutes, and directed the driver to take me to the correct railway station; I would take the train to Agra, and join the tour there. I went into the waiting room to

find the tour director. He gave me my ticket, and told me that I
would be on car B, and that the train would be here in five minutes.
I went out of the door to the train platform and stopped in horror!
The platform was covered with bodies! I gasped and stood still for a
full minute. Most of the people were sleeping; a mother was nursing her baby. There were all kinds of people: men, women, children,
and babies, all huddled together, covering the whole train platform!

When the train came into the station, I had to step over legs and
bodies to get to car B. With the help of one of the conductors, I
managed to reach the train and get aboard. It was like our old fashioned parlour cars, with only about twelve lounge seats, and it was
cool and fresh. I felt exhausted, with mixed emotions. As the train
pulled out of the station, sleeping people were stirring, and children were running around and jumping over the sleeping bodies. It
was a very sad sight! I did not notice the scenery, except that it all
seemed so dry, with yellows and browns dominating. Most of the
trees were not large, just short and shrub-like. We seemed to be
passing through one small village after another, stopping at one
crowded little station after another, finally reaching Agra. The tour
bus was waiting for us at the station. It was very, very hot!

The bus was very crowded, and I had to sit in the back seat. It was
hard and slippery. Even the metal rod across the back of the seat in
front of me was too hot to touch. The driver would jam on his
brakes, and all of us on the back seat would slip to the floor if we
did not hang on to something. It was a rough, winding road, and I
was so miserable that I could not remember what we were supposed to see.

Finally we were taken to an air-conditioned restaurant. I determined that I would not get back in that awful bus. But after I had
eaten and had a cold drink, I decided that I must see the Taj Mahal;
it was not very far now.

As I sat on the steps of the building at the Taj Mahal gate, I was glad that I had come. It was a dramatic sight. The four minarets were like a frame of a picture, and the garden and pool set off the central mosque. When we entered the mausoleum, we had to take off our shoes. The white marble floor in the entrance was very hot. We all ran into the beautiful interior of this amazing building.

Emperor Shan Jahan built the Taj Mahal between 1631 and 1653 for his wife, who died in childbirth. It was a study of perfection. Every piece of white marble was set perfectly. Every white square was perfectly matched. The coloured inlay work was delicate and artistic. The alcoves and the ceiling were decorated with matching designs. The inlaid jewels and semi precious stones provided lustre and brilliance. It was a sight to remember forever, and I was very glad that I had come.

Back in the hotel that evening, I decided to take my gift list to the fabulous brass shop. I had a wonderful time choosing the brass for one family, and other things for other families. I had gift cards ready and used the envelopes to write the names and addresses for each gift. The manager of the shop assured me that they would take care of all of the mailing and postage. (Everything arrived, and to all the correct people. My great-grandchildren are still using some of the stools.) Then I went back to the jewellers to buy a few more gifts, which I did not ship home. It was wonderful to go through my gift list. I had not wanted to carry anything more in my already full luggage. I had concluded that the shops in the first class hotel would be trustworthy. I went to bed that night feeling pleased with my purchases.

The tour to the city of Old Delhi the next morning was an anticlimax, but interesting. The old tour bus lumbered down the streets of the ancient city. Most of the streets were too narrow for vehicle travel, but our driver managed to manoeuvre his bus into the courtyard of the Red Fort. The high and solid Red Fort wall enclosed a rare mixture of buildings. Some of them dated back to 600 B.C. There were temples and palaces, mosques and many other old buildings. I saw the building that the Grand Mogul had presided over; it had jewel encrusted walls. The Hall of Private Audience had beautiful white marble walls. The palaces dated back to the time of the Moguls. After that we went to the Great Mosque Jama Masjid; it was spectacular, and seemed to be competing with every other mosque as the most decorative. I was filled with awe.

Back in the hotel, I checked with the airline about my flight to Bangkok, Thailand. I was flying out the next day. All was in order, so I took a refreshing cool bath, and rested until my friend, Laura Lambert, the woman I'd met in Iran, picked me up. There had been a note in my key slot confirming the invitation to dinner that evening, and saying that I would be called for at six.

The Lambert's house was large and looked English, but the interior had a spacious oriental style. My hosts were vegetarians, and the tables were covered with dozens of dainty, pretty arrangements of a wide variety of delicious foods. I resolved to remember some of the decorative arrangements to use when I had a buffet dinner at home. It was delightful to feel among friends when I was alone and half way around the world. They introduced me to some very interesting guests. Two of the young ladies were involved with the Experiment in International Living. They were Italian, and were in New Delhi living with one of the Lambert's neighbours for a month. We had a good time talking about mutual friends in Italy. They were also involved with the Experiment. It was great fun, and I had enjoyed myself. My host kindly drove me home to my hotel.

The airport, next morning, still had the numerous boys anxious to carry my luggage. This time I was ready, and managed to have one boy carry my two bags to the check-in counter. As I checked in, I realized that I was happy that I had cancelled my trip to Mysore. I had wanted to see Bill's project (an educational institute built with F.A.O. money), but it would have meant an hour flight to the south, another hotel, more sightseeing and another flight back. And more airport struggles. I was happy to be leaving India. The crowds were overwhelming, and the heat was exhausting.

We flew over golden-brownish land for what seemed to be hours. Gradually I realized that the landscape, 32,000 feet below, was no longer hazy, but looked clear and very green. We were flying over Burma, then approaching Bangkok over water. The landing was good, and the customs and immigration officials were kind, gentle, and efficient, and taxicabs were available.

My first view of the Erawan Hotel was breathtaking! The magnificent oriental style building was set in the most luscious, beautiful tropical gardens that I have ever seen. The entrance lobby was set well back from the road, seeming to be an extension of the garden. I was happy that my room was on the ground level, looking out over more gardens and a swimming pool, and that my room was air-conditioned, after the long hot taxi drive. The swimming pool looked very inviting and I needed a day to relax, so I decided to cancel my trip to Cambodia, where I had booked a tour to see the Ankor Watt Temples, and spend the extra day here. I enjoyed a leisurely soak in the warm pool, looking up at the blue sky and the glorious flowers. It was too hot to linger at the pool side after the swim, so I returned to my room, which seemed freezing. I dressed quickly and went out to the lovely garden room lobby—a restful place to sit and read my tour pamphlets.

I wanted to visit T.I.M. land, and booked a tour. The letters stand for Thailand In Miniature, and it is exactly that. The tour bus called for me at ten the next day. It was a fascinating morning. Inside the decorative gateway were small exhibits of things to see in Thailand. Our group wandered around fascinated. I learned about the life of the silk worm: it takes twenty-eight days for the worm to come out of the cocoon, and then it begins to eat mulberry leaves and spin its silk gossamer thread, which is spun into thread for weaving into beautiful silk cloth. The snake pit was also fascinating, with different kinds of poisonous snakes, and a fat boa constrictor. A man convinced us that it was not dangerous by draping it around his neck! I was not impressed, nor could I be persuaded to try one around my neck! I turned away quickly to see the dancers in the outdoor theatre.

Children from the orphanage were dancing, and the guide told us that these children learned to dance to earn money. Later, we came back to see the young girls performing their rather stiff, formal, stylized dance. Beyond the theatre, water buffalo were plowing the flooded rice fields. These animals were domesticated and trained to be useful, sometimes being used for milk. During the rice exhibit tour, we were told about the different kinds of rice and how it has to be planted in flooded fields with plenty of water and heat until it is ready to be harvested.

The last, and most exciting exhibit, was the one where we watched the domesticated elephants. We all sat in comfortable chairs watching these huge animals working with the mahout sitting on their backs giving them instructions by touch and commands! It was wonderful to see them pick up a teak log with their trunks, carry it to the edge of the water and then roll it into the water. After the elephant show ended we all returned to our tour buses.

That afternoon I did a little exploring on my own in the city centre. I did not feel strange or threatened, and realized how much more relaxed I had become about travelling on my own. There did not seem to be many high-rise, modern office buildings, but very lovely interesting small shops. The silk shops and jewelry stores were most popular. I lingered, tempted to buy at least seven different pieces of the most beautiful silk that I have ever seen. I resisted, planning to see the weavers at work later in the day. During my walk through the city I met a troop of Boy Scouts in traditional uniforms. I stopped to talk with them but they could not speak English. One boy said, "Canada," pointing to my Canadian pin and hugged himself with a shiver, meaning cold. I spread my arms waving them around saying, "Thailand. Hot!" We all laughed.

Our communication was uninspired, but they walked away waving and smiling. My two boys had been Scouts, and I would have liked to have been able to talk to these happy looking young Scouts.

The dining room at the hotel was delightful. Although the tables were set formally, the room was designed to look as if you were dining in the garden. Two sides were open to the garden, and plants and flowers were everywhere. The food was Thai in character, with lots of peanut sauces and curries. The waiter spoke English and explained some of the dishes to me. I enjoyed the mild curry seafood and rice and the coconut dessert. I lingered over my coffee, reluctant to leave this lovely garden room. I did, however, go to bed early as the confusion of time changes had left me ready to sleep at odd hours, and the next day was to be a busy one, with a river cruise in the morning and the King's Palace and Temples in the afternoon.

Next morning, I was driven to the small wharf, where about twenty people waited for the sightseeing launch to take us up the River Chao Phraya. Waiting with us were a couple of Buddhist monks with shaved heads and saffron robes. This was my first sight of men of this religion. Young men enter the monastery for one or two years, giving up all worldly goods. They live in these saffron robes, shave their heads, and live by donations (we would call it begging). We left the saffron robed young men behind us on the dock.

The river was wide and deep. Ocean going ships could sail up to the perimeter of Bangkok, but not as far as the historic Oriental Hotel. Our landing was north of the hotel. The river was alive with boats of all sizes and descriptions. We were only a medium sized launch holding about twenty tourists.

It was an astonishing trip up the river. The river was like a street, with houses built with their front steps going right down into the water, and often a boat would be tied up to the tiny landing. There was something happening at most of the houses. A mother was bathing her baby in the river, another washing clothes, a man was carrying pails of water up into the house. Then there were boats of all kinds called floating markets that sold fruits and vegetables. Other boats were delivering groceries, or mail. Some of the people were trying to sell things to the tourists. One couple came down the steps of their house, dressed for the city, calmly stepped into their motor boat, started the motor, and sped down the river to the city.

After a few miles of solid rows of houses, the river widened to look like a small lake. The scene became even livelier and more colourful. Here there were more markets on the shore as well as on the river. It was hard to tell which were floating and which were on land. A floating refreshment boat tied up to us, selling cold drinks and ice-cream. I could distinguish a carpenter and a tailor shop on the shore.

We went farther up the river until we came to a tributary, where there was a small park on the point. As we tied up to the wharf, we could see that the park extended inland. On the shore, an elephant stood waiting to take people for a ride. None of our passengers accepted the offer. We turned around here and floated down towards town. Where the river had widened, we found ourselves in a river traffic jam. We had to inch our way though this confusing mass of boats. It was a relaxing few minutes. Nobody seemed to be in a hurry. There was much laughter and gentle pushing of flower markets, fruit markets, and tourist launches.

Some of our passengers wanted to have lunch at the Oriental Hotel so our tour guide tied up at the hotel dock. I joined them, having lunch with a view of the activity on the river.

After lunch I joined a tour going to see the Grand Palace and the temple where the Emerald Buddha was on view. The tour bus stopped for us to see the royal barges. They were huge canoes, like Hawaiian outriggers, elaborately decorated with ivory and gold.

A watt, a holy place of worship for the people of Bangkok, Thailand. It was located in the Imperial Palace grounds.

Many Chinese live all their lives on one of the small junks. A boat built specially for the Chinese waters. Here they are tied up in rows, and I called it "Junk city".

Elephants working at TIM land (Thailand in Miniature) located near Bangkok. These are domesticated elephants controlled by the Mahout, by sound and touch. They were getting the elephants to roll logs into the water.

They were used on special occasions. I wondered if these ancient relics were still seaworthy. The ornate building seemed to be in the same area as the Grand Palace, which we were not allowed to enter.

We wandered around the elaborate temples, religious statues, and watts, which were solid pyramid-like structures for worship. The watts varied in size, the larger ones being fifteen feet in diameter and about thirty feet high and the smaller ones measuring about ten feet in diameter and about twelve feet high. I walked in and out of temples and around watts taking pictures until my feet could not manage another temple. But the door to the temple of the Emerald Buddha was opened, so I took one last lingering look at this huge statue.

One of the smaller temples reminded me of the miniature ones that people put up on a pedestal at the corner of their gardens, looking a little like a bird house. The occupants place offerings to the gods at the foot of the watt to keep away bad spirits. The gifts could be flowers, food, or any other small donation. I had my camera with me, and had taken a whole roll of pictures, knowing that they could not really show the beauty or magnitude of this fabulous collection of temples, watts, and royal buildings.

As I dragged my feet out to the street to find a taxi, I wished that I could have come back with the guide. He could have further explained the difference between a 'temple' and a 'watt'.

The taxi was slow as it threaded its way back to the hotel. When I arrived back, I added a flower to the offerings at the wee temple at the corner of our hotel garden. I had time to rest my weary feet before going for another delicious meal in that delightful dining room. I checked over my tickets, vouchers, and traveller's cheques, ready for my early morning flight to Hong Kong.

HONG KONG

The Cathay Pacific Airline was luxurious, the seats comfortable, the stewardesses charming, and the meals delicious. The arrival in Hong Kong was terrifying. We seemed to be flying between apartment buildings and I thought the pilot was going to land on a downtown street! I could look into the window of an apartment that seemed just a few feet beyond the tip of the plane wing. We did land safely. Customs, immigration, and currency exchanging were efficient, and the limousine taking guests to the Mandarin Hotel was waiting by the cab stand. We inched our way through the traffic jams of Kowloon, magically missing bicycles and pedestrians, vendors carts, and rickshaws.

Our first destination was the car ferry. As we drove up the ferry ramp, I gave a sigh of relief. We had not run over anyone, or crashed into a rickshaw! The ferry ran between the mainland and the Island of Hong Kong. The Mandarin Hotel is near the harbour front in the city of Victoria. Our driver seemed to know what he was doing, and he delivered us at the door of the majestic

Mandarin Hotel. The reservation was verified, and I was ushered up to a beautiful room on the fourth floor looking out over the harbour, and Kowloon. The view from my room was fantastic. To my left the harbour widened, and was alive with every kind of floating boat, barge, ferry, little junks, big junks, sailboats, row-boats, ocean liners, and, on that day, an American warship.

I wanted to get started immediately on my next voyage of discovery. As it was late afternoon, I would be limited to short jaunts. The busy little pedestrian ferry to Kowloon caught my attention. As I walked over to the ferry ramp, one was ready to leave, so I found my Hong Kong coins, paid the ten cents, and went across the harbour to Kowloon. After walking around for awhile I discovered that the attractive building in front of me was the famous Peninsula Hotel. When I went in, English tea was being served in the pleasant lounge. What a delightful surprise, just in time for me to rest my feet. A very British waiter showed me to a comfortable chair and handed me a menu. The Earl Grey tea, served in delicate china cups and saucers, was refreshing. The tiny sandwiches, tea biscuits and cakes were delicious. I would have liked to linger longer, but it was getting late. I did not want to be in this crowded city of Kowloon after dark.

I found my way back to the ferry, and for an additional ten cents, returned to Hong Kong. As I departed the ferry, I noticed a long line of rickshaws and their drivers waiting for customers. Long ago I had been repelled by the practice of human beings pulling other humans in rickshaws. However, having watched these clever drivers weaving their way in and out of the traffic jams in the narrow streets and alleys, I was converted. Conveniently, I crawled into one and returned to the Mandarin. The doorman helped me out as if I was stepping out of a stretch limousine.

It had been quite a day, leaving Thailand that morning, having tea in the Peninsula Hotel in Kowloon, and now having to decide where to eat dinner. I did not feel like tackling the hotel dining room. Studying my pamphlet, I found that there was a coffee shop attached to the hotel, so that's where I went.

The tour bus trip next morning to Kowloon and the New Territories was confusing because we went from the peaceful bustle of Hong Kong to its border with Communist China, and the Red Guard. I was picked up at my hotel, and we crossed over to Kowloon on the car ferry. As we wound in and out of the narrow streets, the guide pointed out speciality shops, banks, and the historic Peninsula Hotel. We turned inland, away from the harbour, into the countryside of the New Territories. It seemed to take a long time to leave the city and the old and new apartments and shacks behind us. Near the border, we went through a very ancient village with such narrow streets that we could not pass a car. When a car had to back up to let us pass, the local inhabitants were very hostile.

We left the village behind, climbing up a long hill overlooking the Pearl River, the end of the Territories. Right there in front of us was the impenetrable barrier separating us from "Red" China. There was a large turn-around area, with an extensive tourist complex of shops, a coffee shop, and washroom facilities. At that time the Red Guards were running the country on the other side of the barricade. There was a lot of violence and killing. But the river looked so calm and peaceful, and the little farm on the island in the middle of the river looked so normal, with ducks and geese swimming in and out of the water. It seemed incomprehensible to believe that the Red Guards were causing such havoc in Canton, only a few miles up the river from this peaceful farm.

At this traffic end of the road there was a typical tourist shop, where I joined the crowd browsing around looking for souvenirs. The usual wood models of Chinese junks were attractive. I bought one and looked at other carvings. In the corner, I found a carving of Confucius. It was a lovely intricately carved ebony statue approximately ten inches tall. The impulse to buy this lovely statue on the border of Red China was impossible to resist. I expected that it would be too expensive, but the clerk said six Hong Kong dollars were equal to five Canadian dollars. I bought it. I carefully wrapped my fragile treasure in lots of tissue paper and tucked it into the bottom of my suitcase. (When I arrived home, the customs thought it was valuable and wanted twenty-five dollars duty!)

On our way back from the border, I asked to be dropped off at the Peninsula Hotel where I had a light lunch and browsed in the hotel arcade shops. During our morning tour of the city I had seen a good-looking department store not far from the hotel. It was very modern and full of interesting merchandise. While I was browsing around, I could hear this continuous clicking noise. It seemed to come from everywhere. "There must be a lot of nervous people, clacking beads together," I said to myself as I looked around. As I watched the lady in front of me, I realized that they were all using the abacus to add and subtract for their bills. I was impressed. The rumour was that this particular store sold goods smuggled in from Red China.

I walked to the ferry and had a short rest on a bench before venturing up to the top of Hong Kong Island by cable car. The view at the top overlooking the cities and the Territories was extensive. On one side I could see the harbour, almost as far as the ocean. Below us were the two cities, Victoria on the Hong Kong side, and Kowloon spreading almost as far as the eye could see. The harbour widens on the Kowloon side, and in this area is Junk City, where hundreds of junks are tied to long wharves or to each other, row after row. Further to the left is the mouth of the river and numerous islands.

As it was getting dark, I returned to my hotel and decided to go to the main dining room on the top floor for dinner. When I arrived, I was taken to a nice table by the window. As I stepped into the room, I stood still in amazement. The tables and chairs were arranged in an orthodox way, but everything else was exotically oriental. The brilliant colours in the decorations, and the gorgeous silk and satin costumes of the ladies seemed more like a stage setting than a hotel dining room. I finally realized that the waiter was trying to show me to a table by the window. The view was fabulous. Outside, the lights of the two cities twinkled like fairyland. The dark harbour was alive with lights of boats of all kinds, the noble passenger ferries chugging back and forth, Junk city, and a large American navy ship anchored to the left of the ferry dock. Inside, the scene was equally dazzling. In the centre was a magnificently carved black ebony table inlaid with mother of pearl. In the centre of the table, a huge silver bowl held the largest bouquet of fresh flowers that I have ever seen. Most of the guests wore evening clothes. The women were a mixture of Oriental and Western occidental, some in Oriental style silks, and some in Paris style silks and satins. I do not remember what I ate, but I did have a problem with my chopsticks! It was a gala evening. I left regretfully.

The tour boat waiting for me the next morning was unique. It had been built to resemble a Chinese junk, but was large enough to hold about thirty passengers. We toured the local docks, went around the American warship—at a respectable distance, then crossed the harbour to see Junk City. There were hundreds of junks, large and small, tied up to wharves, or to each other. Families lived on these boats all of their lives. Some of the people were fishermen, and some worked on the mainland. There was a women hanging out a washing, a man pulling up a pail of sea water to scrub the deck. It was a puzzling sight. No one could answer my questions about their fresh water and food supplies. Our tour guide spoke the minimum amount of English.

As we rounded the tip of the island, the squatters living on the rocky cliffs caught my attention, and then the city of Aberdeen came into sight. I cannot imagine any city that could be more unlike Aberdeen, Scotland. Though we did not go onto the shore, we could see the light coloured wooden houses tucked into the rocky hillside. The other Aberdeen has large granite buildings, solid brick or stone houses. The harbour here was very colourful.

Boats of every kind filled the bay. Our tour junk tied up to the huge floating restaurant where we were to have lunch. We were ushered up to the top deck, where the tables were all set, ready for lunch. It was a set menu, and various dishes were brought to us, one after another. Some were delicious. Some unfamiliar, looking like squid or octopus. It was like eating on a cruise ship surrounded by the sea. Our tour junk was waiting for us, and the trip back to our loading dock was very pleasant.

There was not much daylight left, so I took the faithful ferry over to Kowloon, did some more exploring in and around the Peninsula Hotel, had tea again in the lounge, and confirmed my reservations for the flight to Japan early the next morning. On the ferry going back to the Mandarin Hotel, I decided to take one last look at the arcade boutiques in my hotel. They were on the third floor and extended out across the street and into the office building behind the hotel. The shops were full of fabulous jewelry, watches, bolts of silks and satins, lacquer ornaments inlaid with mother of pearl, and many other interesting things. I finally tore myself away, returned to my lovely room, and sorted and packed for the flight to Japan.

JAPAN

As I flew out of Hong Kong's Kai-Tac Airport, I studied my itinerary for my visit to Japan. I was happy to see that I would be staying at the Hilton Hotel, in Tokyo. Some people criticize the Hilton chain, but I have found it excellent. I know that the toilet flushes; the hot water comes out of the hot water tap; the bed is clean and comfortable.

The flight and taxi ride to the hotel was, thankfully, uneventful. I checked in and asked for a taxi to pick me up in one hour so I could do some shopping in a fabulous downtown department store. On the way to the store, I saw the famous Imperial Hotel and the busy railway station. When I arrived at the store, I was particularly impressed with the charming young woman who stood at the bottom of the escalator answering questions in English. I visited the departments which intrigued me, but it was getting late, so I returned to my hotel in time to try out one of the many restaurants.

Next morning, I was scheduled to go on a tour to Nikko, (a national park north of Tokyo). It was a delightful change from shopping. The bus wound around and around the hairpin turns up to the temples and shrines. The beautiful Kegon waterfall made a dramatic back drop for the many buildings and parks. We crossed over the river to the largest temple. We all stood admiring the brilliant green and red roof with the sweeping corners drawing your eyes up to the sky. Over the steps leading into the temple a dramatic frieze of three monkeys was cut out of stone: one with his paws over his ears, one with them over his eyes, and the other covering his mouth, depicting the lesson "to hear no evil, to see no evil, and to speak no evil." As I descended the wide steps, I came face to face with what seemed like a hundred children. This mass of children with black hair, whites shirts and dark pants was looking up at me. It unnerved me. I felt ten feet tall and very alien. Next time I will wear a black wig and dark contact lenses.

I walked to the pretty red bridge and stood looking at this wonderful scene of unforgettable beauty. I wanted to get a picture of the magnificent panorama of temples, shrines, and pagodas, with the glorious mountains, Kegon waterfall, and luscious green trees. I realize that for me, personally, an artificial picture was not so important. My memory of this beautiful restful scene will always be vivid.

We returned in time for me to do some window shopping before dinner. I was fascinated with the kimonos. At first they seemed heavy and cumbersome, unlike the saris of India. (On the streets, most of the people wore western clothes.) The lacquer work was beautiful, but the jewelry shops attracted most of my attention. The setting of pearls in elaborate jewelry was exquisite. I knew that I would be doing some serious shopping before I left Japan! I resisted temptation, returning to the hotel for a delicious Japanese dinner.

The Hilton had a special room for tempura cooking and serving meals. In the centre of the room was a high, oblong counter seating about twenty people. Inside each end, a chef produced the delicious, delicate tempura food. Depending on what you ordered, he would dip the vegetable, seafood, or meat, into the light batter, then into the simmering oil to cook. Your order would be served to you — take out — on a hot plate, delicious, crispy, and crunchy. It was fun to watch these two super chefs. I never saw them falter, or mix up an order. The preparation of the food was fascinating to watch, and the food itself was satisfying.

I spent the next day seeing Tokyo. The innumerable temples and shrines, the Palace, government buildings, the station, the high speed 'bullet' trains, the old historic Imperial Hotel and the downtown area were overwhelming. I returned to my nice quiet room exhausted.

The next morning, I joined a five day bus tour to the south. Our first call was to see the 720 year old Bronze Buddha, the Daibutsu, in Kamakura. To get there, we had to drive through the port city of Yokohama. This Buddha was very impressive. As we climbed up the mountain highway, we were all stretching our necks to get a glimpse of the famous Fujiyama Mountain. Luck was not with us that day. It rained and rained, and misty clouds surrounded the whole area.

The charming Hakone Resort Hotel looked very inviting. It was chilly in the mountains, and the glowing fireplaces seemed to welcome us. We were happy to settle in for the night. Delicious smells were coming from the dining room. The dining room was down a few steps from the lobby and looked very delightful with the rustic wooden tables and chairs carved in the Oriental fashion. The lamps and Japanese lanterns gave the room a cosy festive glow. We had a choice of a western or Japanese style meal. I chose the sukiyaki (pronounced, see akee.) It was very interesting. I looked at the raw egg on my dinner plate with misgivings. In front of my plate, they placed a piping hot bowl of chicken and vegetables, cut in bite sized pieces, similar to a stew. The ritual was to take a piece of the very hot chicken or vegetable and dip it into the cool egg, making it cool enough to eat. After the first cautious dips, I enjoyed the sukiyaki very much, forgot about the rain and the dripping wet trees, and enjoyed the friendly cheerful atmosphere and the strange but delicious meal.

In the morning, we started off in damp cloudy weather, winding through and down the mountains on a road with many hairpin turns. At one of the sharpest turns, there was a huge double mirror reflecting the traffic coming the opposite way. Suddenly the clouds lifted and there in front of us was the magnificent Mt. Fujiyama! We were at the right place at the right moment! The bus pulled onto the side of the road, and we all filed out to get a better view. Some were taking pictures, but I thought we were too close for a good shot. Other busses and cars were joining us. Although the rain had stopped, the clouds were gathering again, and Mt. Fuji was disappearing.

Our route led us up over the pass and down into Atami. The bus dropped us off at the Bullet Train station. Our train tickets to Kyoto had numbers on them, and we were told to stand at those numbers. When the train pulled into the station, it would stop, matching the numbers on the cars with the numbers painted on the platform. It did exactly that! If I was standing at 423, the train would stop, and the door marked 423 would open exactly in front of me. Everybody with 423 on their ticket would get in quickly because the train stopped for only two minutes. It was a clever idea and worked very well. We all managed to get on safely, and we were off to visit Kyoto for three days.

Kyoto was a new experience. The hotel Miyako was unique, being built on a hillside. The lobby, dining room, and reception were on one level. To get to the bedrooms, we had to go up four or five steps, where two doors led to the bedrooms on this level, then up four or five more steps, with another hall leading us to more bedrooms, and so on up to the back of the hotel. I was glad that this hotel did not have Japanese-style sleeping arrangements. I did not think that sleeping on a tatami mat on the floor would be very restful after a day of sightseeing.

At dinner I enjoyed a new dish, which I called Mongolian Hot Pot. The food was cooked at the table in the boiling broth, in a circular trough. The centre 'chimney' must have been used for the smoke to escape when the fire was real. Everyone put his or her vegetables or meat into the broth until it was cooked. Some of the results were peculiar!

It is impossible to describe all of the wonders of Kyoto. But the innumerable, spectacular temples and shrines were so colourful and dramatic, they dominated the scenery. Here and there between the temples and shrines, we came to other interesting shops, warehouses and factories. The silk weaving illustrated more clever art work. In the back alley, behind the silk weaving plant, we found a stream with yards and yards of silk floating in the water. The mineral in the water would set the dye. Then there were the dolls, beautiful dolls of all kinds and sizes. I was convinced that all the examples of artistry displayed in the creating, designing, and producing of such beautiful dolls and gorgeous costumes would make Kyoto famous. If possible, the lacquer work and the delicate china outshone the dolls in artistic glamour. We wandered back to the hotel through many winding narrow old streets. I was very impressed with the cleanliness of these well worn old lanes. No donkeys were allowed, no vehicles could squeeze through, only people and hand carts. We arrived back in the hotel overwhelmed with the artistic beauty that we had seen. The Golden Temple was the most memorable sight. It seemed to float over the landscape as if floating in the sea. The landscape garden was a perfect setting for this magnificent structure.

Reluctantly, we left all of this fascinating city behind us, and set out for Nara. The city of Nara was old and had many temples and shrines, but what made Nara so unique was the park. There was a huge temple housing the largest Buddha in the world. The lawns in the park were extensive and small deer were roaming free, enjoying the attention of the tourists. For a few pennies anyone could buy a bag of deer food and the animals were tame enough to take the treats out of the hands of the people. Some of the deer became quite aggressive in their attempt to get more than their share. I soon got rid of my bag of treats and moved away from these beautiful but aggressive creatures. There was an archway that led to a peaceful wooded area of the park. I enjoyed the change of pace, and spent the rest of the time wandering through this lovely park.

On our way back to the bus we stopped to admire the pagoda with its large square base and upward sweeping curves at each corner of the roof. A pagoda usually has three or five stories with balconies around each floor. In Nara the five story pagoda was particularly attractive. As we went back past the 'biggest Buddha in the world', we wondered how many people could stand on the upturned hand! It was so big!

We returned to Tokyo the next morning on the superb Bullet Train with many hundreds of other travellers. The next day would be my last chance to do my shopping. I had a wonderful time buying presents for my family, and some lovely things for myself. In a small tourist shop near the railway station, I found a gorgeous kimono coloured creamy white and lined in red silk with three elaborately embroidered large birds in gold, silver, red, and green.

My next visit was to the Mikimoto Pearl Emporium. It was too grand to be called a shop. The pearls were set in all kinds of imaginable pieces of jewelry and decorative objects. The brooches, earrings and necklaces attracted most of my attention. After spending more than an hour admiring the gorgeous display, I bought a few small gifts for the family, and a pretty brooch for myself. During the earlier part of my journey, I had mailed my gifts to my family and friends. This saved me carrying them around the world and helped me keep within my quota for customs declarations.

When I arrived back in my hotel room with my purchases, I realized that my luggage would have to be re-packed in order to hold my beautiful kimono. Finally I squeezed the things that I would not need into one bag so that I could check it right through to Vancouver, including my bulky kimono.

HONOLULU

The flight to Honolulu turned out to be a particularly memorable one. When I arrived at the airport, I was astonished to see the new (at the time) 747 airplane standing in the loading zone, and excited to find that I was going to be flying on that huge plane! It looked as big as a three-story building. How was it ever going to take off, I wondered? Sitting in my seat inside, I felt reassured; it felt so solid. The stewardesses were walking around so naturally, passing out magazines and checking to see that all seat belts were fastened. The take-off was smooth, and after flying through a few clouds we levelled off at 32,000 feet.

A few hours later, the captain announced the Apollo spacecraft had landed on the moon! Everyone was very excited. Here we were so high in the sky over the middle of the Pacific Ocean feeling half way there ourselves. When the next announcement came over the loud speaker: "Neil Armstrong has stepped down onto the moon!" cheers reverberated through the plane! It was an unforgettable moment. The excitement, and the friendly chatter made the trip seem shorter—and we landed in Honolulu a few hours before we left Japan! We had crossed the dateline and gained a day while they were landing on the moon. It was July 20,1969, 10:56 eastern daylight time.

I was booked into the new Kahala Hilton Hotel, and arrived late. The ringing of the telephone woke me up the next morning. A familiar voice said, "Hello, Mom." I sat up quickly, wondering where I was. It was my son, Doug's, voice! "Oh, Doug, where am I, and where are you?" His answer was astonishing. "You are in Honolulu, and I am in Dawson Creek, B.C., and if you hold on, I will let you talk to your daughters, Pat in Toronto and Daphne in Vancouver." After a few strange noises I was talking to the three of them, thousands of miles away. I was wide awake now, and very excited. They all sounded as if they were in the next room! It was wonderful to hear their dear voices after an absence of nearly three months. I suddenly realized I had become very homesick. We talked family talk for a precious few minutes, then they said, "good-bye Mom. See you." I sat there clinging to the phone until funny noises forced me to hang up. Staying over in Honolulu had seemed to be a good idea so many months ago, but now I wanted to be home.

However, after one look out of the window at the beautiful flowers, the magnificent palm trees, the blue sea and sky, I wanted to go out, smell the warm sea air, and feel the warmth of the Hawaiian sun. I had arrived late the night before, so I was anxious to explore the hotel and the beach. The hotel was on the east end of the Island of Oahu, which is one of the Hawaiian Islands. Honolulu is the city, and Waikiki is the popular beach where the main resort hotels are located. The area around the Kahala Hilton was mostly residential, with a lovely golf course stretching past the hotel up to the foot of the mountains. The front of the hotel faced the ocean, looking across the strait to Molokai, another island in the Hawaiian chain. The big Island of Hawaii, Maui, Kauai, Oahu, and several small islands are all in the State of Hawaii.

A reef protected the lagoon in front of my hotel, making swimming from the sandy beach very pleasant for the more timid swimmers. The hotel also had a beautiful pool, and a huge artificial lagoon close to the hotel where they trained the dolphins that performed for the guests.

After exploring the area and having a swim in the pool and the ocean, I watched the dolphins performing. After lunch, I walked to the new shopping mall, about a mile away. The shops were very American. I admired the Hawaiian shops and bought a muumuu. I love the muumuu, finding it the coolest dress for that climate. Later that afternoon I caught the Hilton shuttle bus that takes hotel guests from this hotel to the Hilton Hawaiian Village, my favourite hotel, at Waikiki beach. It was like a homecoming. I had stayed there on many trips and had many happy memories. As I walked through the lobby and into the picturesque garden and stood admiring the goldfish in the pretty pool, I wanted to rush back to the registration desk and move in. It was getting dark and they were lighting the torch lights around the garden. By now the beach was almost deserted. After dark the beach is not so inviting, so I had a snack in the coffee shop and took the shuttle bus back to the Kahala, resolving to return for breakfast.

In the morning I did return to the Hawaiian Village, and had a sentimental breakfast by the sea. I started with half a papaya, then had banana pancakes with coconut syrup, my special delight. I lingered over my coffee wishing that I could stay on the beach lounging under one of the colourful umbrellas. Looking east, towards Diamond Head, I could see that there were many changes on the shores of Waikiki. The cement breakwater in front of the R & R Complex—built during the Second World War for soldiers to come to for 'rest and recreation'—was still there. When our family had visited Honolulu, we'd stayed at the Hawaiian Village, and the walk on the breakwater to the Royal Hawaiian Hotel was a daily excursion.

At the moment, the tide was in, so the waves were dashing against the rocks in front of the breakwater, splashing over the walkway. (These rocks have now been hauled away, replaced with tons of sand creating another lovely beach.) Later as I lingered over lunch in the Royal Hawaiian, I remembered a rainy cold December day in 1931, when I was twenty-three years old...

My mother, father, and I were about to cross the Pacific to Honolulu on the Empress of Asia. There was an orchestra on the dock, streamers, flags, bouquets of flowers, and crowds of people saying farewell. The special farewell was for the Canadian delegation going to Honolulu to meet New Zealand officials to draw up a Trade Treaty between the two countries. My Father was Canada's Minister of Trade and Commerce, and he would represent Canada. The Prime Minister of New Zealand, the Rt. Hon. Downie-Stewart, would lead the New Zealand delegates to Honolulu. The conference would be held in the Royal Hawaiian Hotel.

On the way to Victoria, British Columbia, our only stop before Honolulu, I explored the ship. It seemed very big and very glamorous. After docking in the outer harbour of Victoria, we sailed out through the Strait of Juan de Fuca.

Mother, Dad, and I were seated at the captain's table for dinner. But as we rolled into the rough seas of the Pacific Ocean, I became very seasick! Unfortunately, I remained that way until we arrived in a warmer and calmer sea on the day before arriving in Honolulu, on Christmas day. A walk on the deck and a rest on a deck chair, revived me enough to attend the evenings entertainment, the Christmas Eve farewell dinner and dance. Magically, the formal dining room had been converted into a festive Christmas Eve party room, with the traditional Christmas tree decorated and lit up with coloured lights. It was a gala celebration.

We were due to dock in Honolulu at nine, Christmas morning. The Customs and Immigration officials were to board the ship early, so that we could have the routine over before landing. We passed Diamond Head about eight. It looked like a mountain thrusting out into the sea. Then I got my first glimpse of Waikiki, and what a beautiful, unforgettable picture it made! The curve of the white beach with the large pink Royal Hawaiian and the smaller white Ala Moana Hotel dominated the scene.

The impressive vivid green mountains were the backdrop. The deep blue of the sky hung over it all. The sea was many shades of blue and turquoise with the crests of the waves snowy white as they rolled into shore. We could see the smaller Outrigger Clubhouse, and a few other small buildings and cottages clustered along the shore. I was really excited about getting there at last. After finishing with formalities, we were allowed to go out on the deck. We had docked at the Aloha Tower Wharf. Things were happening out there. At the prow Hula dancers were swinging grass skirts, musicians were playing, and singers sang the songs that told the stories about the Hula dance.

Officials were arriving to welcome us, and Dad was a gracious greeter and receiver of the welcoming committee. Now the flower ladies were coming on board, greeting everyone with a lei and a kiss on each cheek, looking like flowers themselves with their colourful muumuus and flowers in their hair. The Hawaiian greeting was "Aloha", as they placed the flower lei around the neck. Soon the formal and informal greetings were over and we were ushered off the ship.

We had just passed the Aloha Tower, when we were overwhelmed with more flower ladies in colourful muumuus with more leis. Finally, we were able to get into the waiting limousines. Our route took us past the small fishing wharves, then through the Ala Moana Park, an extensive grassy area stretching from the sea to the beginning of Waikiki. (Now there is a spectacular shopping centre there, known as the Ala Moana.) We went over a little river on a small wooden bridge. The wee stream poured out into a wide marshy area before joining the sea, and the driver told us that we were now in the district of Waikiki. After passing a few small cottages, we turned into the extensive gardens of the Royal Hawaiian Hotel.

These were Depression years, and there were not many other guests in the hotel, so the arrival of fifteen or twenty from our ship did not bother the efficient staff.

We were very happy with our suite of rooms, which looked out over the spectacular Waikiki Beach. There were fresh flowers, bowls of unfamiliar fruit, and a small but real fir Christmas tree in our living room. The tree had come on our ship and had been rushed to our suite and decorated for our arrival! As we unpacked, we put our presents under the tree. After lunch we had a little ceremony and opened our presents. We found it hard to believe that it was Christmas day.

When we had finished our lunch, we were taken on a tour of the hotel and garden. The halls were tiled in vivid shades of blue, turquoise and green. Lounges and terraces were open to the gardens and the sea, and decorated in the same blue colours. (Now, in 1969, I stand in carpeted halls, and the rooms are closed and air-conditioned.) The extensive gardens surrounded the hotel, stretching to the sea on the south, to Kalakaua Avenue in the north, and beyond the driveway in the west. Impenetrable hedges of palm trees, banana palms, plumeria, hibiscus, bougainvillea, and other flowering shrubs surrounded the hotel giving it privacy. Our own private beach joined the Waikiki beach, which stretched past the Outrigger Club House and the lovely Ala Moana Hotel to the public park. I was particularly interested in the private beach, as I love to swim.

As my Dad would be very busy during the days of the conference, we decided to go for our swim every morning at six-thirty, before he had to join the others for breakfast. It was great fun. The sea was warm, but the air could be quite chilly as we dashed in for our breakfast, after our swim.

The New Zealanders arrived on Boxing Day. The Prime Minister, Rt. Hon. Downie-Stewart, was permanently confined to a wheelchair, and had a valet to take care of his personal needs. His sister, Miss Downie-Stewart, acted as his hostess and his personal secretary. She was always there to make the arrangements for meals and conference meetings.

While the men were busy during the days, the Hawaiians arranged outings for the women of the two countries. One day we visited a pineapple plantation where we saw the pineapples being harvested, and then we were taken to the Dole pineapple factory. When we visited the factory, we were very impressed with the way nothing was wasted. The tops were used to start another plant, the outer prickly skin was used for fertilizer, and the tough core was squeezed for the acid. The women sorted the fruit for size and quality. Then as the fruit was moved down each floor, it was ready for canning. It was a very modern factory, and was one of the first to provide lunch rooms and facilities for the working mothers. On each floor as we came down we were invited to help ourselves to the chilled pineapple juice from the large containers ready for anyone—taps and paper cups provided. I had taken special notice of the pleasant atmosphere in the factory, and drank the ice cold juice on every floor.

I had been included in the guest list of officials from both countries who were to dine with the Doles. However, at three that afternoon, I became very ill. The doctor arrived and diagnosed my problem as too much pineapple juice mixed with a lunch of crayfish. He prescribed a cure, but I missed the dinner party. It was, probably, a fortunate thing that I did not arrive there for the dinner party, because the Doles had provided a 'child's high chair' for me, as Dad had asked if he could take his "little daughter" with him. I can imagine their embarrassment when Dad and Mother would have arrived with me. The Hawaiian entertainment committee did a fabulous job; almost every evening they arranged dancing, singing, and story telling, often out in the garden by the light of the torches.

One night the moon was full and the Hula girls looked especially graceful as they told stories with their hands and bodies. Occasionally men would join in the dances, and they would perform famous Hawaiian war dances and chants. Some of the male dancers were prisoners who were out for the evening on a pass. Crime had not been such a problem because there were not many ways to escape from the Island.

One of the interesting day trips was by car to the Pali Pass. My mother and I drove up to the high pass, but the road stopped there. You could look down over a precipitous cliff, thousands of feet down. The warriors forced their enemies up and over, dashing them to their deaths. (Now there are two multi-lane tunnels taking people to the other side of the Island in minutes, instead of the hours it used to take going around by the coastal road.)

One of the most exciting events during Christmas week was the arrival of a ship from Japan with the all-star Canadian Rugby Team returning triumphantly to Canada. They had a twenty-four hour stop over in Honolulu. The entertainment committee decided to hold their 1931 New Year's Eve Ball for the team. It was a gala party! The committee took over the Ala Moana Hotel Ballroom, decorating it like a fairyland with flowers, streamers, and the colourful flags of the countries involved. The hosts and hostesses had invited some lovely young women, and the Hawaiian Hula dancers made the evening festive and fun for our boys from the rugby team. The ballroom of the Ala Moana extends out to the beach with windows opening out onto a veranda.

Strolling out to catch a breath of the glorious fresh sea breeze between dances was delightful. (One of the interesting young men that I met that night, John Rowland, was later to become manager of my husband's Toronto office. Another young man, Burt Sutherland, from Vancouver, who was in our trade delegation, met John Rowland as well, and years later became a member of my husband's Vancouver staff. The two men and their wives were very important in our lives, and were great friends)...

I finished my lunch, and decided I wanted to see if the ballroom in the Ala Moana Hotel was still there. It was there, just as I remembered it. The French doors still opened onto the wide veranda, and the magnificent banyon tree was still in the courtyard, much bigger, with many more side branches. I sat under the banyon tree and remembered that happy evening, and the happy days that followed. I stood up and walked down to the beach, watching the surfers riding the waves into the sandy beach. In 1931 there was only an occasional surfer, but now there were dozens. It was fascinating to see so many manage to stay up and others falling. I had tried once, on another visit, to ride the surfboard, but had never managed to stand for more than a second. I was happy that I could paddle back to the beach safely.

It was time to return to the Hilton shuttle bus. I walked back; going through the shopping mall that has been built on the former Royal Hawaiian Hotel gardens. There were two floors of very interesting shops, but I resisted the temptation to buy any more gifts. I was curious to see how they had managed to build this large mall without ruining the gardens. I walked through a side entrance to the hotel and sat on the steps leading to the gardens. They had done a beautiful job of replanting the border, partially obscuring the buildings of the mall. It was hard to remember that the garden had extended one city block long, to Kalakaua Avenue.

I returned to the Kahala Hilton for a short swim before dressing for the special Bali dinner, with Bali dancers for our entertainment. The dancers were very beautiful, but I prefer the lovely, graceful Hawaiian dancers.

Next morning I caught the early shuttle to the Hawaiian Village to, again, have my favourite breakfast and look out over the beach to Diamond Head. When I had finished my morning treat, I took the sightseeing bus to the Bishop Museum. This is a very interesting exhibit, giving us a bird's eye view of how Hawaii was discovered and of the original people who settled the country. The courage of those seafaring men and women who travelled by catamaran canoes over thousands of uncharted miles of turbulent ocean filled me with awe. I always see the arrival of the missionaries with mixed feelings. Their descendants are probably now wearing muumuus and bikinis on the beach. I visited the missionary houses on the Sunday after going to the Kaluawai church. Part of the service is in the Hawaiian language, and I liked the quiet rhythm of the hymns.

The view from the church over the Ala Moana Park to the colourful sea and the blue sky was very lovely. The solid stone church, with the mountains in the background, was impressive. The missionary houses looked small and primitive, unsuitable for the Hawaiian climate. Their lives could not have been very easy. After a short visit to the Ala Moana Shopping Centre to finish my gift shopping, I returned to the Hawaiian Village for a light dinner. With a last look at the view of Diamond Head, I walked through the lovely gardens to the shuttle bus, and returned to the Kahala Hilton. The limousine to the airport was leaving at seven next morning for my return flight to Vancouver via San Francisco, so I took one last look at the beautiful lagoon and pools, and went to my room to pack.

As I finished packing, I was full of confusing feelings. Homesickness had swept over me in Japan, and I was very excited about getting home. But I loved Hawaii, and I was leaving it with regrets!

On the plane to San Francisco, I remembered the trip home, via San Francisco, in 1932.

The New Zealand Prime Minister, and my father, the Canadian repre-sentative at the trade talks, had agreed on the terms and wording of the treaty, and they were ready to return to their respective countries to have the treaty ratified by their parliaments. The New Zealanders were able to get accommodation on a ship leaving in two days. We were advised that there were no ships sailing to Canada for two WEEKS. This was bad news as there was urgent business needing attention in Ottawa, and the treaty had to be ratified before it could become law. The leaders of the Canadian delegates discovered that a Japanese ship, the Shinyo Maru, was sailing to San Francisco on the next day -but, no luck!

No foreign ship was allowed to carry passengers from one American port to another American port. We appealed to the American officials. Their reply was, "No, it is the law. Only the President of the United States of America can give permission." Telegrams were sent to our Prime Minister, Rt. Hon. R. B. Bennett, to ask the U.S. President to grant us permission to sail on the Shinyo Maru. Finally, permission was granted! We said, "Aloha," and sailed late the next afternoon.

The Shinyo Maru was a Japanese cargo and passenger ship, sailing from Japan to San Francisco with one stop in Honolulu, where most of the passengers terminated their journey. Our Canadian group filled most of the available space. Because we had obtained special permission from the President, we were assumed to be very special, and we were treated like royalty. Sometimes it was very embarrassing, and frustrating. Very few of the crew could speak any English, and would bow deeply and back up into the nearest doorway, as we would approach. It was especially embarrassing when a crewmember would back into the entrance to the bathroom, where I was rushing to relieve my seasickness.

After a few days, I found that I was not so nauseated if I spent most of the time out on the deck. The weather was sunny and warm, and the sea was calm. On the third evening the captain had a special Japanese dinner on the deck of the ship. The tables were set about one foot high, on matting. The guests were to sit cross-legged on the matting. Cushions were brought for the women, and we sat side-saddle on the cushions. Knives and forks were provided for most of the Canadians who could not use chopsticks. Innumerable pretty dishes with colourful, elaborately decorated foods were placed in front of each guest in endless succession. At that time, I was not familiar with Japanese food, feeling that I should not eat the pretty flowers, although they assured me that everything served on our plates was edible. It was a great introduction to the formality of a Japanese dinner, and a taste of their cuisine.

When I woke up on the last morning, the cabin was in confusion! The ship was rolling in a peculiar way. The bow of the ship would rise up, and chairs, luggage, and any loose objects would slide back. There would be a pause, then everything slid forward. I dressed in a hurry to go out to see what was happening. It was unbelievable! We were caught in the aftermath of a violent storm. The waves were huge. Our ship would ride up the mountainous wave, falter at the crest, then plunge down the other side of the wave. I was very happy to see the cliffs of San Francisco. When we docked, there was a considerable delay because of the unusual arrival of Canadians on a Japanese ship from Honolulu. "It is not allowed!" said the angry official, but his reception of us changed dramatically when he read the documents from the President. Reporters swarmed around us delaying our landing. My father was able to handle the questions. "Why were you in Honolulu? Why were you on a Japanese ship? Why? Why?" endlessly. One of the reporters cornered me, asking about a murder that had occurred in Honolulu around New Years.

I was asked, "Did you go out alone at night? Were you afraid?" I answered that I was not afraid in Honolulu, that I did not usually go out alone at night when at home, so why would I start going out alone in Honolulu?" I was horrified when the evening paper came out with front page headlines, "Canadian Cabinet Minister's daughter afraid to go out alone in Honolulu." "Honolulu not safe for ladies to go out alone!" I had not had much experience with reporters, but I soon learned the words, "No comment."

Finally, we were ushered into a limousine and taken to the St. Francis Hotel, where we were given the Presidential Suite. Our luggage had been brought up from the ship, and arrived there before us. After lunch we were taken on a sightseeing tour of the city. Our tour guide took us up Knob Hill; we watched the cable cars going up over the hill and down to Fisherman's Wharf; we saw Golden Gate Park and the sight where the Golden Gate Bridge was going to be built. The Presidio was Navy property, and had been used as a refugee hospital after the 1906 earthquake. The fire that followed the earthquake destroyed the downtown area, from the waterfront to Vaness Avenue, which, being very wide, stopped the flames. There were very few signs of the ruins after all these years, but the horror stories were very much alive. We went back to the Golden Gate Park for a short walk to get rid of the feeling of having sea legs.

Next morning, we boarded a train for Seattle where we were met by official government cars, as we would miss the connection to Vancouver otherwise. My parents returned to Ottawa and I remained home in Vancouver to resume my teaching career...

Now I was flying into San Francisco from Honolulu on a 747 jet airliner. With only a short wait, I boarded a flight to Vancouver. I had travelled around the world and now I was heading home. The words of a song, "Be it ever so humble, there's no place like home," were never truer.

THE END

Mother, Dad, and I in Hawaii in 1931.

ISBN 155212419-3

9 781552 124192